MW00778588

The Drama of Metaphysics

An Exploration into the Psychological Power of Worldviews

Stephen Alexander Beach

En Route Books and Media, LLC
Saint Louis, MO

Make the time

En Route Books and Media, LLC

5705 Rhodes Avenue

St. Louis, MO 63109

contactus@enroutebooksandmedia.com

Cover credit: Sebastian Mahfood

with Flammarion Engraving

© 2022 Stephen Alexander Beach

ISBN-13: 978-1-956715-46-0

Library of Congress Control Number:

2022936340

Table of Contents

In honor of Paul Cole Beach

"It is very important here to identify these two separate and antagonistic forces [the individual thing and the universal form] battling ceaselessly in conscious thought, thus producing a perennial drama of ideas..."

-- Jose Ortega y Gasset

Introduction

The history of Western philosophy has been a conversation that has lasted over two thousand years. It is a conversation that has been focused on understanding the mysterious nature of being.[1] From the Pre-Socratics' speculations on nature to Berkeley's idealism, the central philosophical question has always involved something to the effect of peering into reality and asking, *"What is it?"* Until the 19th century, a core tenet of philosophy was that there is a duality in things. There must be a principle in things to explain the reality of change, and another principle to explain the reality of identity.[2] While change was seen in the physical world, the identity in things was held

---

[1] Jose Ortega y Gasset, *The Origin of Philosophy* (New York: W.W. Norton Company, 1967), Ch 1.

[2] Everyone is familiar with the example of Heraclitus' river. It is physically changing all the time, yet its identity is the same in that it is the same river.

to be a mysterious[3] aspect of reality that transcended the senses.[4] This immaterial identity pro-

-----

[3] Ortega y Gasset, *The Origin of Philosophy*, 59.
"For what we have of the thing, when we have its name,
is a caricature: its concept. And unless we proceed with
caution, unless we evince distrust for words and attempt to pursue the things themselves, the names will
be transformed into masks, which instead of enabling
the thing to be in some way present for us, will conceal
the thing from us. While the former is the magical gift
of words, their feat, the latter is their disgrace, the thing
language constantly verges on - a masquerade, a farce,
mere jabber."

[4] Jose Ortega y Gasset, *What is Philosophy?* (New
York: W.W. Norton Company, 1960.), 82. "The usual
expression of the problem is the question "What is this
or that thing?" Note the strangeness of this mental act.
That thing about which we ask, "What is it?" is there,
in one sense or another it has being; otherwise, it
would never occur to us to ask about it. But it follows
that we are not content that it exists and is there - on
the contrary, we are disturbed that it is there, and is of
this or that kind; its existence irritates us. Why? Obvi-
ously because what it is, as it is, is not sufficient in itself; on the contrary we see that if it is only what it
seems to be, if there is nothing else behind its appearance which completes it and supports it, its being is incomprehensible; or to put it another way, its being is
not a being but a pseudo-being, something which

vided much of the impetus for philosophical exploration, most especially related to the mystery of the human experience, which is likewise subject to this change/identity dichotomy. The exploration into the mystery of the human person has produced three fundamental questions which are ever present in human life. *"Where have I come from?"*, *"Who am I?"*, and *"What is the ultimate purpose of life?"* In other words, man is always trying to find an answer to the problem of his origin, his identity, and his ultimate purpose.[5] The problem that man runs into in answering these questions is that reality confronts him with incomprehensible complexity. The only way man can function in his daily life is to create boundaries that simplify his world. He must shut out unnecessary complexity by having some type of answers to these questions. Without these at least

---

ought not to be. Hence there is no theoretic problem unless it proceeds from what exists, what is indisputably there, but which nonetheless is thought of as not existing, as though it ought not to be."

[5] Pope John Paul II, Encyclical on The Relationship Between Faith and Reason *Fides et Ratio* (14 September 1998), §1-6.

preliminary answers, human beings would be unable to act as they would be frozen in the ultimate version of the paradox of choice.[6] Every person forms these answers, whether they are conscious of it or not, by living inside a type of story. Man must participate in a grand narrative that guides him in the face of the mysteries of life. With that grand narrative providing answers to his needed sense of origin, identity, and purpose, he is then able to act.[7] This is not just true on the individual

---

[6] Jose Ortega y Gasset, *The Idea of Principle in Leibnitz and the Evolution of Deductive Theory*. (New York: W.W. Norton Company, 1971), 272. "...The system of our occupations is secondary to the system of our theories, of our convictions as to what things are; the 'knowing what to do' is founded on 'knowing what is.' With more or less adjustment the system of actions in each stage of human progress is fitted into the system of ideas and oriented by them. A variation of any importance in our opinions has very great repercussions on our actions."

[7] Jose Ortega y Gasset, *Some Lessons in Metaphysics*. (New York: W.W. Norton Company, 1969.), 27. "Man's life seems to be made up of situations, just as matter is composed of atoms. As long as one lives, one is living in a specific situation. But it is evident that just as all these situations, however different they may be, are vital, so there will be in them an elemental, basic structure which makes all of them situations within the

level, but on each level of the human community: the family, the city, the political, and the religious. These stories are shared.[8] They provide the means by which people can be drawn together in authentic communion through the sharing of common goods and beliefs.[9] The absence of such a shared story is also responsible for alienation between people, for the labeling of the other as unknown and enemy. These stories regulate more about one's life than most are ever consciously aware of.

---

realm of man. ... And we say that metaphysics consists of the fact that man seeks a basic orientation in his situation. But this assumes that man's situation - that is, his life - consists of a basic disorientation. This is not a matter of man's finding himself, in his own life, partly disoriented in this or that respect ... But our definition presupposes a total and fundamental dislocation; that is to say, it is not that man happens to be disoriented, to be losing himself in life, but that, insofar as one can see, man's situation, his life, in itself *is* disorientation, is being lost, and therefore, metaphysics exists."

[8] Antonio Moreno, *Jung, Gods, and Modern Man* (Notre Dame, Indiana: University of Notre Dame Press, 1970), 4.

[9] Karol Wojtyla, *Love and Responsibility* (New York: Farrar-Straus-Giroux, 1981), 28-30.

These grand narratives have been around as long as humanity. For most of history, man has lived inside the story of the "book of nature," expressing answers to the human experience in pagan religious ritual and rational philosophical formulations. At a privileged time in history, though, man received a new book. He received the revelation of the Word of God, recorded in the Jewish and Christian Testaments, an event which split history in two. Since the time of that split, for two thousand years the Western world has lived within the Christian story, one which clearly casts human origin, identity, and purpose within the light of the transcendent and metaphysical reality. However, something transpired in the 19th and 20th centuries that convinced man that the Christian story was not real. The average citizen was told that the story's author did not really exist and that the characters in the story were actually the true authors. He was told that man had the power to rewrite all the previous chapters of human existence and to alter the storyline to a new ending.[10] As expressed by theologian Hans

---

[10] Ortega y Gasset, *The Origin of Philosophy*, 101. "Just as the aforementioned cause separated men from

Urs Von Balthasar, man cast aside the "Theo-
Drama" for the autobiography of the "Ego-
Drama." This ego-drama was not written in a
holy book, but written on man's own paper, in his
own ink, and by his own hand. In the words of
19th-century Russian novelist Fyodor Dostoyevsky's progressive atheist character, Kirilov:

> He who will conquer pain and terror [leaving
> behind the Christian past] will become him-
> self a god. Then there will be a new life, a new
> man; everything will be new... then they will
> divide history into two parts: From the gorilla

---

tradition, so this surrender to worldly life uprooted
him from religion. All the consequences incumbent
upon the former were carried to the extreme: amid a
life of abundance man was left uprooted, dangling in
mid-air. He floated amid the aerial element of his
mounting possibilities. This was the inevitable coun-
terbalance. The stability and vital security of an individual's existence were not automatically and effort-
lessly bestowed upon him by innate adherence to an
unquestioned tradition, but the individual himself
with total awareness had to fabricate a foundation, a
terra firma to support himself. Hence he had no
choice; using the fluid, ethereal matter available from
existing possibilities, he had to construct for himself a
world and a life."

to the annihilation of God, and from the annihilation of God to... the transformation of
the earth, and of man physically. Man will be
God, and will be transformed physically, and
the world will be transformed and things will
be transformed and thoughts and all feelings.[11]

Every story has power over the individual
man who exists within it. The question becomes:
Is that story a fairytale, or a nightmare? The goal
of this book is to explain how the nightmarish
events of the 20th century were possible because of
the abandonment of the traditional Western metaphysical and theistic story, and its replacement
with naturalist, nihilist, occultist, and communist
ideologies. This will be done, first, by exploring
the power of "weltanschauung," or worldview,
which these collective stories wield over the psyche and actions of the individual man and woman
who exist inside them. Hannah Arendt's work is
valuable in this regard, especially her analysis of
the corruption of Germany in the 20th century.

---

[11] Fyodor Dostoyevsky, *The Possessed*, Kindle.
116, 119.

Second, the core tenets of the worldviews of the 19th and 20th century which sought to replace Metaphysical Theism as the dominant worldview will be described. This will include their new claims for man's origin, identity, and purpose. Included in this will be an analysis of Metaphysical skepticism, Methodological Naturalism, Nihilism, and Communism. A key thread will be shown among these worldviews; that they all reject the mystery of identity in things, closing themselves off to metaphysical reality. Third, the argument will be made that while Metaphysical Theism can be suppressed, it can never be destroyed, as it is a fundamentally constituent part of reality.[12] This argument will be taken from the work of the 20th-century Spanish Existentialist philosopher Jose Ortega y Gasset. Finally, this book will have a heuristic value in that it will provide an insight into the ever greater rift occurring in the West between the worldviews of Metaphysical Theism and Scientific Progressivism, taking the form of the Transhumanist Movement. It will conclude with a warning that, unless humanity regains its shared narrative, the destructive forces

---

[12] Ortega y Gasset, *What is Philosophy?*, 21-3.

of the 20th century will continue through the 21st and will be followed in successive centuries by even graver consequences.

Chapter I

The Power of Worldviews: Finding a Sufficient Explanation for the Horrors of the 20th Century

The transition from the 19th to 20th centuries was certainly one of the most tumultuous periods in modern history. The Industrial Revolution had brought Western society out of the old structures remaining from the Middle Ages into a new age of technological potential. The countryside was being left behind for the cities. The power of the traditional aristocracy was being placed into the hands of wealthy businessmen. The old forms of government were being transformed by theories of new political systems. The influence of religion on public life was waning as the search for answers was less directed towards the priest and more directed towards the scientist. Many of the old religious and philosophical belief systems were beginning to be seen as burdensome.[1] There was also a rapid growth in technology which provided a major increase in people's daily quality of life and bodily health.

At the same time all this was happening, technology was also providing the means by which the most shocking horrors in human history were perpetrated. Everywhere across the globe mass genocides took place as a result of the spread of new ideologies, mostly in the forms of Communism and Fascism. The death toll in the 20th century was almost equal to the death toll of all previous centuries combined.[2] People were not just killed in the usual means of the past. There were novel methods of murder and social manipulation that emerged from man's psyche.[3] Some examples include the demonization of entire groups followed by mass genocide, the use of mass-produced mechanized wea-pons of war,

---

[1] Henri De Lubac, *The Drama of Atheist Humanism* (San Francisco: Ignatius, 1998), 23-5.

[2] Chris Hedges, "What Every Person Should Know About War." *The New York Times* (NY), July 6, 2003, What to Read. at www.nytimes.com.

[3] Hannah Arendt, *The Origin of Totalitarianism* (New York: Harcourt, 1970), 461.

and the implementation of methods of propaganda which sought to control the minds of the population. Every person must recognize that this is *what* happened in the 20th century.

The question that this chapter seeks to understand is *why* it happened, and psychologically *how* the perpetrators were able to accomplish such evil. What changed to make countries that had traditionally been Christian suddenly become heralds of mass genocide?[4] This is what

---

[4] Timeline - World History Documentaries. "How An American TV Crew Tracked Down a Nazi. Nazi Hunters." YouTube video, from Timeline - World History Documentaries. Posted by Timeline - World History Documentaries on 3 October 2021. At https://youtu.be/hu42C7rinEU

Take for example, Erich Priebke. Priebke was a high ranking SS officer stationed in Italy during the Second World War. In a certain incident in 1944, thirty three Germans were killed in a bombing. As retaliation Priebke was told by Hitler to execute 330 Italians. They actually rounded up 335 people and led these people into the Ardeatine cave where they were put on their knees in front of a pit. They were shot in the back of the head in groups of five, their bodies pushed forward into a heap down in the pit. Priebke began the massacre by shooting the first two men, having his guards finish the rest. Eric Priebke was able to escape to Europe after the war and live out the rest of

needs to be explored in the philosophy of world-views.

Defining "Worldview"

The answer to the question of rapid ideological transformation lies in the power of "weltanschauung," or worldview. A worldview refers to the most universal set of beliefs about reality to which a person ascribes. As was mentioned in the introduction, because reality is so far beyond man's understanding, there are a core set of questions that every person exercises some amount of

───────────────────────────

his life in Argentina. In 1994 an ABC news crew found Priebke, and in a candid moment on the street got him to talk. He had just left his post at the German school to take his lunch when they came up on him. They asked him the question whether he felt guilty about what he did back in the war. His reply was simply, "That was our order. You live in this time, but we that lived in 1933, it made sense. That was not a crime. Yes today, but not at this time. Many young people do things that when they are old men they are very sorry about." What is one to make of the undoubtedly countless examples of men and women like Priebke from the War? Were these countless cogs in the machinery of genocide all themselves monsters, or could there be another possible explanation?

faith in answering. Accepting certain answers to these fundamental questions casts every other one of life's questions and situations within an understandable framework. One is able to reason from those beliefs as first principles to come to conclusions regarding every lesser set of data that one encounters in life. In short, it is an agreement to a set of first principles about the very nature of reality which makes action possible.

As time passes, and man's knowledge of reality grows, there will be less faith needed in positing certain first principles as they will be known with more evidence. Yet it does not seem possible that the need for worldviews will ever disappear. To remove the need for them would require that man know everything about everything. Man would need to have mastered the mystery of existence so thoroughly that he would even have the knowledge of how to create being from nothing.[5]

---

[5] Joseph Cardinal Ratzinger, *Introduction to Christianity* (San Francisco: Ignatius Press, 2004), 59. "... in the Italian philosopher Giambattista Vico (1668 - 1744), who was almost certainly the first to formulate a completely new idea of truth and knowledge and who, in a piece of bold anticipation, coined the typical

Only in creating something from nothing will complete knowledge be had about the thing.[6] Man would truly have to be God, as God has no belief system, only knowledge. This will never be the case for man as belief will always be necessary regarding certain fundamental realities which he experiences only indirectly.

---

formula of the modern spirit when it comes to dealing with the question of truth and reality. Against the Scholastic equation *verum est ens* (being is truth) he advances his own formula, *verum quia factum*. That is to say, all that we can truly know is what we have made ourselves."

[6] Ortega y Gasset, *What is Philosophy?*, 82. Ortega y Gasset also expresses this idea as the completion of all rational inquiry, to understand the genesis of being so thoroughly that one can unwind its existence back to its non-existence. "Theory, then, and let us emphasize the extravagance of this - begins by denying reality, by virtually destroying, annihilating the world; the ideal is to draw the world back into nothingness, to what it was before creation, since it is surprising that it exists, and the aim is to trace again the path of its genesis. If, then, the practical problem consists of making what is into what is not, but would be convenient if it were, the theoretic problem consists in making what is not into what is, and which in its present form irritates the intellect with its insufficiency."

So far in history certain central controversies have presented themselves and risen to the top of man's philosophical consciousness. In answering the fundamental question of the nature of being, man must grapple either with a belief in the existence of metaphysical forms or of continuous material flux. He must find out if the Principle of Sufficient Reason is true and reality is rationally intelligible, or if reality is based more in an emotional experience of the will. In answering the questions of the origin of everything, he must affirm or deny the existence of God and of the Judeo-Christian history of man. In answering the question of man's identity, he must believe that man is body and soul or that he is just a body. He must grapple with the possibility of a universal common good, or of a society where there can only be the will to power. In answering the question regarding the purpose of everything, man is forced to choose between a view of man that is teleologically ordered towards the transcendent Absolute or a view of man whose future earthly utopia is shaped through social engineering.

This is not to say that the contradictory answers to these fundamental questions are equally

true and that one must simply choose their preference of belief. Philosophy is the rational attempt at providing the *most* correct story about
human existence. At the same time, this does not
mean that those more correct answers cannot be
forcibly suppressed in favor of lesser or incorrect
answers. In fact, the desire to do just that is always
present in the human temptation for power.

The Psychological Power of Worldview

Why is the proclivity to manipulation ever-
present in human society? The answer lies in the
power that belief systems wield over individual
men and women. The way that one views the
world plays a large role in determining how he or
she acts within it. To give people answers to the
great perennial questions of life is to influence
their origin, identity, and purpose. So, if someone
can impose their worldview on others, then they
can control them in a way that exceeds any type
of external coercion. It is a type of coercion from
within the person, as one has restructured how
they see reality. If someone is not aware that this
restructuring has taken place within his or her
mind, he or she may become an unknowing, or

unconscious, servant to the worldview.[7] At that point, the person may even be beyond reach, as all contradictory experience or data will be explained away in light of his or her ideology.[8]

---

[7] Yuri Bezmenov, interview by G. Edward Griffin, "Soviet Subversion of the Free World Press," 1984, available online at American Media, https://youtu.be/jMnhSBySKto. Yuri Bezmenov, a KGB propaganda agent and defector to the West, explained in an interview in the 1980's that the term for this type of person they used was the "useful idiot."

[8] Ibid., "[To] change the perception of reality of every American to such an extent that despite an abundance of information that no one is able to come to sensible conclusions in the interest of defending themselves, their families, their communities, and their country. It's a great brainwashing process which goes very slow and is divided into four basic stages. … You are stuck with them. They are programmed to think and react to certain stimuli in a certain pattern. You cannot change their minds even if you expose them to authentic information. Even if you prove that white is white and that black is black you still cannot change the basic perception and logical behavior. In other words, [for] these people, the process of demoralization is complete and irreversible. … Most of it is done by Americans to Americans because of a lack of moral standards. As I said before, being exposed to true information does not matter anymore because a person

As an example of how opposing worldviews can have the most diverse logical conclusions for human society, consider different answers to just one fundamental question. *Is the story of existence given to humanity, or created by humanity?* If it is given to humanity, then it has a set nature that *should* not be transgressed. If it is created by humanity, then everything about how humans live can be questioned. To make this point clearer, one can put it another way, either Christ is the savior of mankind, or one of Dostoyevsky's characters, Kirilov, is. If one chooses to follow Kirilov, one will arrive at quite different conclusions than from following Christ. Kirilov, who was a social scientist, was studying the reasons why men *did not* kill themselves more frequently. He concluded his research with the idea that history had reached a turning point with his generation that

---

who is demoralized is unable to assess true information. The facts tell nothing to him. Even if I shower him with information, with authentic proof, with documents or pictures. Even if I take him by force to the Soviet Union and show him concentration camps he will refuse to believe it until he is going to receive a kick in his fat bottom."

would reinterpret the meaning of all human history. What was transpiring? Kirilov's generation was the first to realize that God does not exist.[9]

> "'I am bound to show my unbelief,' said Kirilov, walking about the room. 'I have no higher idea than disbelief in God. I have all the history of mankind on my side. Man has done nothing but invent God so as to go on living, and not kill himself; that's the whole of universal history up till now. I am the first one in the whole history of mankind who would not invent God. Let them know it once for all.'"[10]

For Kirilov, all that exists of God is the fear of him that has been embedded into the human psyche. It is embedded so deeply that it is as though God were a million pound stone that hangs above every man's head. The stone would instantly kill

---

[9] Dostoyevsky. *The Possessed*, 116, 119.
[10] Ibid., 116, 119.

him, and he would feel no pain, yet the fear of the stone causes him much grief.[11]

Kirilov is sure that there will be no judgment or afterlife, but it is difficult to rid himself of the fear of God. Thus, he and others of the first generation of atheists must be the saviors of mankind and again split history in two by living out this discovery. "But one, the first, must kill himself, for else who will begin and prove it? So I must certainly kill myself, to begin and prove it."[12] Instead of the God-Man Jesus Christ reordering history, these "man-gods" were trying to accomplish it by embracing their fear and willingly killing themselves. In doing so, they hoped to show that God had no power over them. They hoped to free man's psyche from fear.[13] These saviors

---

[11] Ibid., 116, 119. "'Imagine a stone as big as a great house; it hangs and you are under it; if it falls on you, on your head, will it hurt you?' ... 'A stone as big as a mountain, weighing millions of tons? Of course it wouldn't hurt.' The most learned man, the greatest doctor, all, all will be very much frightened."

[12] Ibid., 677.

[13] Ibid., 677. "I will begin and will make an end of it and open the door, and will save. That's the only thing that will save mankind and will re-create the next

would also free mankind from any belief in good or evil. Man will realize that all that exists is what exists; there are no values. And when there is nothing left to strive for, time itself will cease, and the eternal utopia will arrive on earth.

> "'Life exists, but death doesn't at all.' 'You've begun to believe in a future eternal life?' 'No, not in a future eternal life, but in eternal life here. There are moments, you reach moments, and time suddenly stands still, and it will become eternal. ... When all mankind attains happiness then there will be no more time, for there will be no need of it, a very true thought.' 'Where will they put it?' 'Nowhere. Time's not an object but an idea. It will be extinguished in the mind.'"[14]

Here, one can see where the power of worldview comes from. How far are Kirilov's conclusions about the nature of reality than the

---

generation physically; for with his present physical nature man can't get on without his former God, I believe."

[14] Ibid., 253.

Orthodox Christianity of Russia at that time? Humans do not think in purely individualistic terms.
Human epistemology is something that is shared.
Humans share a common biological nature with
the same drives, motivations, desires, and emo-
tions. Humans share a common psychological
and spiritual nature which manifests itself in universal archetypes. The structure that each person
has given to their attempt at making sense of human origin, identity, and purpose is not unique to
them. Humans share their belief systems about
the world. These shared structures and beliefs are
so powerful that they are even responsible for
what man values in his very perception of reality.
In the vast landscape of what exists, it is these
worldviews which tell him what to ignore and
what to focus on.[15] Clearly, man does not exist as

---

[15] Jordan Peterson. *Maps of Meaning: The Architecture of Belief.* (New York: Routledge, 1998), 2, 4, 5.
"The world can be validly construed as forum for action, or as place of things. The former manner of in-
terpretation-more primordial, and less clearly under-
stood-finds its expression in the arts or humanities, in
ritual, drama, literature and mythology. The world as
forum for action is a place of value, a place where all
things have meaning. This meaning, which is shaped
as a consequence of social interaction, is implication

an island, but always shares some type of "common world" with others of his same worldview. In the words of Joseph Campbell:

> "The first function [of mythology] is that of reconciling consciousness to the preconditions of its own existence - that is, of aligning waking consciousness to the mysterium tremendum of this universe, as it is. ... This I would regard as the essentially religious function of mythology - that is, the mystical function, which represents the discovery and recognition of the dimension of the mystery of being."[16]

The Process of Destroying a Worldview

It is now clear why worldviews are so powerful, but the question remains, how does one go

---

for action, or-at a higher level of analysis implication for the configuration of the interpretive schema that produces or guides action." pg 1.

[16] Joseph Campbell. *Thou Art That, Transforming Religious Metaphor.* (Novato, California: New World Library, 2001), 3.

about destroying an old worldview and implementing a new one? This question is also tied to
the one presented above regarding how the events
of the 20th century took place. Philosopher Hannah Arendt explicitly shows in her work how this
type of worldview death and rebirth happened
through her analysis of totalitarianism in Germany and Russia at the beginning of the 20th century. Her essential thesis is that with the implosion of the Metaphysical Theistic worldview new
ideologies of total control were put forward in order to force the adoption of a new Materialist
view of reality. This total control was necessary
because otherwise people would not go along
with the radical transformation of society. Even
the traditional coercion of dictatorship was not
enough to accomplish this task. Thus, as was
mentioned above, these ideologies sought to em-
bed themselves so deeply into the individual man
and woman that the result was the formation of a
type of pantheistic collective spirit. This spirit
possessed individuals so thoroughly that their actions, and even their thoughts, were simple logical applications of the ideology to all situations,
not the actions of an individual person.

To unpack her claims in more detail, Arendt begins her thoughts with a positive description of Western Civilization as a reference point. She says that up until the 19th century the West was capable of an authentic understanding of itself because to truly "understand" what a thing is one must have a perspective larger than the thing by which to evaluate it. This larger perspective was the transcendent perspective the Christian West took towards human existence. It was the religious tradition and history of this transcendent perspective that provided the West with an identity as a people.[17] She also characterizes Western Civilization as having political systems that allowed for a common good available for all its members. It allowed for a type of equality that enabled people to live together and participate within a common vision. These laws and equality, based on the traditional natural law, provided a stability to society not subject to the shifting tides of men's desires or feelings. It was this common

---

[17] Hannah Arendt. "The Great Tradition and the Nature of Totalitarianism." (Lecture at New School for Social Research, 1953), at Https://Memory.loc.gov/ Ammem/ArendthtmI/mharendtFolderP05.Html. "Without a past, we are no longer human."

interest,[18] shared by every member that regulated the interactions between people. This common good started within the family and then grew from there into the political realm.[19] The three structures of the common good, religion, tradition, and politics, had been the stable foundations for the West since Roman times. The structures allowed a "common world" to emerge which brought about a common way of living, understanding, and flourishing for its members. In other words, there was an established worldview that was ancient, stable, and successful.

Arendt says that at a certain point in history leading up to the 19th century this worldview collapsed. The traditions were no longer lived, only studied. Religion was relegated into the private sphere. The common metaphysical and theistic worldview was being lost, more and more seen as harmful for its people. For a while, it did not collapse completely as there was a "common sense" that remained in people's minds. Like a ghost of

---

[18] Ibid. Arendt points out that the word "interest" is from two Latin words which literally mean "to be in between" things.

[19] Ibid.

the past, a common sense is a practical memory that hangs on in people's day-to-day lives, reminding them how they were to understand and act towards one another. Eventually, this memory was also lost, and society was at the edge of ideological implosion in the 20th century. This chaos then led to the rapid ascendency of fascist and communist authoritarian control to set things right, as people need that shared worldview to operate in for their daily lives.[20]

On a practical level, Arendt provides an interesting account of the means by which those who were exultant in this new "post-theistic" age in the 20th century sought to destroy the traditional Metaphysical Theistic worldview of the past. The basic method involved stripping the people of their old identity in order to impose a new one on them. The stripping of identity first began with the turning of the traditional class structures into one mass amorphous group. Class

---

[20] Hannah Arendt, "Totalitarianism" (Lecture at Oberlin College, Oberlin, Ohio, 28 October 1954), at www.memory.loc.gov/ammem/arendthtml/arendthome.html. "The truth is that nobody can live outside a common world…"

structures, such as guilds, nobility, or trade organizations, all provided an identity for people within the old society. These structures had to be eliminated so these people would be willing to take their place in the new system.[21] This was begun by appealing to the people who were already at the fringes of society and did not participate or fit into the common narrative. They were the ones without a worldview, waiting to have one imposed on them.[22]

The men from World War I experiencing the effects of physical and psychological brutalization, trench warfare, chemical weapons, and mechanized infantries returned home in a type of actual and ideological shell shock. They were perfectly prepared to receive a new narrative about the meaning of life. The intelligentsia of the time had told them that war was a healthy part of the Darwinian struggle of the survival of the fittest.[23]

---

[21] Arendt, *The Origins of Totalitarianism*, 315

[22] Ibid., 312

[23] Discovery Science. "Darwin, Africa, and Genocide: The Horror of Scientific Racism." YouTube video, from Discovery Institute. Posted by Discovery Science on 7 July 2020, at https://youtu.be/lQPrvPM38Ws

In so many ways the intelligentsia had champi-
oned this "crisis."[24] With mass unemployment,
inflation, unstable governments, and poverty all
piled on, a large section of the population was
completely alienated from the worldview and
structures of the past.[25] These people did not need
convincing arguments to sway them to support a
new type of ideological movement. All they
needed were lies that stoked their alienation. The
ideological elite told the new "mass man" that history was one giant lie because it always excluded
people like them. They were told that the lies were
to control them and to keep them within the
structures of the past. The continued repetition,
combined with their unstable state, proved successful in convincing them that the past, and everything representing it, needed to be destroyed.[26]

---

[24] Arendt, *The Origins of Totalitarianism*, 329.
"This generation remembered the war as the great
prelude to the break-down of classes and their transformation into masses. War, with its constant murder-
ous arbitrariness, became the symbol for death, the
'great equalizer' and therefore the true father of a new
world order."

[25] Ibid., 315-6.

[26] Ibid., 333. "They had convinced themselves that
traditional historiography was a forgery in any case,

Once this mass movement of rebellion began to gain momentum, the materialist elites behind the scenes could finally unmask themselves to applause and acceptance. They were just like the alienated mass man, willing to overthrow everything. Now they could openly show it and present themselves as the leaders of the new movement.[27]

There was a second stage required in this process. The elites needed to find a way to break down those in society who were not alienated, but

---

since it had excluded the underprivileged and oppressed from the memory of mankind. ... To this aversion of the intellectual elite for official historiography, to its conviction that history, was a forgery anyway, might as well be the playground of crackpots, must be added the terrible, demoralizing fascination in the possibility that gigantic lies and monstrous falsehoods can eventually be established as unquestioned facts, that man may be free to change his own past at will, and that the difference between truth and falsehood may cease to be objective and become a mere matter of power and cleverness, of pressure an infinite repetition. ... Simple forgeries in the viewpoint of scholarship appeared to receive the sanction of history itself when the whole marching reality of the movement stood behind them and pretended to draw from them the necessary inspiration for action."

[27] Ibid., 334, 335.

who would hold onto the past with much more vigor. A two-pronged approach was taken that involved hollowing the person into a shell through physical and mental isolation from any community with others. Arendt's term for the successful completion of this was to make a person "uprooted" and "superfluous."[28] Physically, man was separated from his fellow citizens through random acts of terror. Previously, the natural law was rationally implemented by the governmental positive law, now these were transcended by the direct application of the Darwinian laws of nature, a law with no logic in its application. Complete fear set into the population as one could be ruined for no reason at all. This was done in order to prevent people from being willing to stand up together and fight back.[29] Aleksandr Solzhenitsyn details a parallel experience in the Soviet Union in his work *The Gulag Archipelago*. He says how random abductions of people in the most mundane circumstances of life were used to scare the population. One would think

---

[28] Ibid., 475.
[29] Ibid., 465, 473-4.

they were going on a date, or getting into a taxi-cab, only to realize that they were being picked up for imprisonment in Lubyanka prison, unable to see their family for ten years. He asks why people just went along quietly with this abuse. Why did not they shout for help, band together, and re-sist?[30] This is the power of random acts of terror.

To take matters further, so that people could not even share in a type of communion of mind centered around the old worldview, they also sought to isolate people from the reality of their experience and very own thoughts. Once every one of the old standards had been destroyed and each individual had become isolated, even from themselves, then there was no perspective by which to judge anything. There was no means of fighting back.[31] Again, Solzhenitsyn presents a parallel experience in his work *One Day in the Life of Ivan Denisovich*. As a prisoner in the gulag,

---

[30] Aleksandr Solzhenitsyn, *The Gulag Archipelago, 1918-1956 An Experiment in Literary Investigation I-II*. (New York: Harper and Row Publishers, 1974), 8, 15.

[31] Arendt, "The Great Tradition and the Nature of Totalitarianism."

even being able to track the time of day with the sun was a source of comfort. So, the Soviets changed how time was told.[32]

The Process of Implementing a New Worldview

Now that the whole society was physically atomized and mentally isolated, the groundwork had been laid for the acceptance of a new worldview. Arendt clearly identifies the two fundamental constituents of the new materialist

----

[32] Aleksandr Solzhenitsyn, *One Day in the Life of Ivan Denisovich.* (NY: Frederick A. Praeger, 1963), 76. "Then they brought in a can to melt snow for the mortar. They heard somebody say it was twelve o'clock already. 'It must be' Shukhov said. 'The sun's right overhead.' 'If it's right overhead,' the Captain shot back, 'that means it's one o'clock, not twelve.' 'How come?' Shukhov asked. 'Any old man can tell you the sun is highest at noon.' 'That's what the old guys say!' the Captain snapped. 'But since then, there's been a law passed and now the sun's highest at one.' 'Who passed the law?' ''The Soviet Government!' The Captain went out with the hods. But Shukhov wouldn't have gone on arguing anyway. Did the sun come under their laws too?"

worldview. These were the unchanging and inevitable laws that supposedly governed both history
and nature. From Darwin, the West learned that
nature is always striving for the survival of the fittest. From Marx, the West was taught that history
has always been the class struggle between the
rich and the poor. From both men, one learned
that there could be no free individual man; there
was only mankind as a species. Mankind was a
manifestation of nature itself born into a prede-
termined struggle which must take place. The
only question that needed to be asked was
whether someone stood with nature as its executioner, or against nature as its justified victim.[33]
The old laws of the government did not even need
to be changed because these "natural laws" superseded any type of human or political law.[34] These
forces cannot be stopped. They are an unending
and continuous process of purification[35] toward

---

[33] Arendt. "The Great Tradition and the Nature of
Totalitarianism." "What is the role of man? To be the
embodiment [of these laws] and to execute them in order to speed them up."

[34] Arendt, "Totalitarianism."

[35] Arendt, *The Origins of Totalitarianism*, 464. Arendt says that if those unfit to live are exterminated,

the collective mankind embodying nature's truth.[36] What defense does a single man have against the power of history and nature? None. The final stage in the possession was to surrender oneself over as an individual manifestation of the ideology. If it was inevitably true that history and nature were the struggles of the classes and races, then this first principle must inform every part of life. It must become that which guides the individual in the chaos of life.[37]

One might ask why starting from the premises of one worldview is any different than starting from the premises of another? For Arendt, ideology is a type of worldview that is not open to the idea of reality presenting truth. It is not open to personal experience. It takes one or two ideas and uses them as a lens to explain the whole of the world, even to explain away contradictions. Ideology is something like an incomplete worldview

---

then different groups will be found to take their place. If classes are broken down, then others will eventually emerge. There will always be the fit and unfit, the oppressor and the oppressed, the victim and the executioner.

[36] Ibid., 466-7.
[37] Ibid., 468-9.

which is applied in a universal way. It insists that people's experience is not really what is happening. There is always some secretive deeper truth that is to be considered.[38] The deeper truth became a type of "sixth sense." This sixth sense consisted in always and everywhere applying ideological logic to the data of the individual's experience.[39] In the end, all that was left was a type of pantheistic mass. Society became a collection of isolated individuals who were forced into obedience because they could not think or act for themselves.[40]

---

[38] Ibid., 470-1; and cf., 336. "...the totalitarian movements asserted their 'superiority' in that they carried a Weltanschauung by which they would take possession of man as a whole."

[39] Ibid., 471-2.

[40] Ibid., 465-66. "It substitutes for the boundaries and channels of communication between individual men a band of iron which holds them so tightly together that it is as though their plurality had disappeared into One Man of gigantic dimensions."

Chapter II

The Worldviews of the 19th and 20th Centuries

It has been shown so far in the previous chapter that the 20th century was a time of worldview collapse, followed by a violent struggle in the implementation of a replacement. The power that worldviews wield over people has also been demonstrated, and thus their inherent ability for the manipulation of populations. This chapter will continue the discussion by seeking to lay out the dominant worldviews which sought to replace Metaphysical Theism in the 20th century. This includes Metaphysical skepticism, Methodological Naturalism, Nihilism, and Communism. Within this analysis a common thread will emerge between these worldviews. Each of them, being faced with the universal philosophical question, *"What is it?"*, seeks to deny the mystery of identity in things. Therefore, the origin, identity, and purpose of human life from which they construct their worldview is one that explicitly denies metaphysical reality, denies God's existence, and is therefore materialist and reductionist in nature. They are worldviews that can only focus on this life. Thus, all these worldviews are driven to reshape human society into a new materialist image, even going to lengths of destruction and manipulation of everything before it, as mentioned in chapter one.

Kantian Criticism as Worldview

Without Immanuel Kant's epistemological skepticism toward traditional metaphysics in the 18th century, it is difficult to see how the famous atheists of the 19th century like Feuerbach, Schopenhauer, Marx, and Nietzsche could have emerged. Since the 17th century, Western civilization had already been descending on an inevitable track for catastrophe because of Descartes' separation of the subjective conscious knower from the objective truth of the world. In the 19th century, at the same time Empiricism was hitting a point of exponential growth, Kant's "Critical Philosophy" made its full impact. It brought Rationalist philosophy to its dying breaths and occasioned the birth of atheism. Theologian Henri De Lubac does not just label these intellectual offspring as atheists, but "anti-theists." They had not refuted God's existence with rational arguments, but willed God out of existence by choice.[1] The ability to "will" such a thing was possible because Kant had given them *supposed* proof that these truths were unknowable; that God's existence, the existence of essential forms in things, the spiritual soul, and teleology were simply speculations, useless, and philosophically unfounded.[2]

To go more in depth on Kant's role in the undermining of the Metaphysical Theistic worldview, it is necessary to understand the basics of Kantian philosophy. Kant pioneered a new school of philosophy which sought to combine what was true from both Rationalism and Empiricism, while leaving behind what was not helpful. The Rationalism of the past he thought to be too dog-

---

[1] De Lubac, *The Drama of Atheist Humanism*, 25.
[2] Ibid., 46.

matic and abstract in the face of the growing empirical sciences. Yet, Hume's skepticism towards
universal truths led Kant even to question the
possibility of scientific laws.[3] Kant, therefore, de-
sired to see what the human mind could know,[4]
thus commencing his Critical Philosophy.[5] In this
philosophy, he was seeking to understand if metaphysical truths, abstractions of pure reason,
could be known or not. Since rationalistic dog-
mas neglected inductive experience, and Hume's
empiricism precluded the possibility of induc-
tively known universal truths, Kant concluded
that truths of pure reason must be present in the
mind *a priori*, only to be revealed through experience. Such a view could bridge both schools.[6]
Kant gave a specific name to this type of truth, the
"synthetic a priori," as it was a truth in which a

---

[3] James Fieser and Samuel Stumpf, *Philosophy: A
Historical Survey With Essential Readings 10th Edition*
(New York: McGraw Hill Education, 2020), page 303.

[4] Ibid., 304.

[5] Ibid., 304.

[6] Ibid., 305. For example, nine times nine was always, and will always be, eighty one. In that sense it is
a priori to the structure of the mind and its judgments
about reality. On the other hand, it took experience of
the world to learn that fact about it.

new predicate was understood to be part of a subject, yet it was also a discovery that it was always
so because of the structure of human understanding.[7]

This was his "Copernican revolution." Instead of Hume's model of understanding, in
which the mind revolved around the facts of the
world by being informed solely by it, Kant's conception reversed this, having the world revolve
around the structure of the mind's perception
and understanding. The mind shapes the experience and reception of the empirical.[8] There are
several fundamental structures of the mind that

---

[7] Ibid., 306-7.

[8] Ibid., 308. "...Kant saw the mind as an active
agent doing something with the objects it experiences.
The mind, Kant says, is structured in such a way that
it imposes its way of knowing on its objects. By its very
nature the mind actively organizes our experiences.
That is, thinking involves not only receiving impres-
sions through our senses but also making judgments
about what we experience. Just as a person who wears
colored glasses sees everything in that color, so every
human being, having the faculty of thought, inevitably
thinks about things in accordance with the natural
structure of the mind."

Kant considers as shaping one's experience of reality;[9] most importantly, rational judgment, which tries to unify the world into intelligible "things-in-themselves." The problem that quickly presents itself is that if there is a structure which is the filter through which reality is perceived, then one can never know the immaterial identity of things as they are, only as they seem. This is his fundamental distinction between the phenomenal and noumenal world.[10] It is also the death of philosophy, as man can no longer even ask the question, *"What is it?"*

What then does one make of the concepts of pure reason which are abstract in nature and have no physical representation? Kant identifies three of these fundamental transcendental truths toward which one must stand in a type of skepticism, while not being able to deny them completely. They are the existence of a unified self, a unified world, and God. Kant considers them reg-

---

[9] These include space, time, quantity, quality, value, relation, and rational judgment.

[10] Fieser, *Philosophy: A Historical Survey With Essential Readings 10th Edition*, 309-10.

ulatory ideas in that they help unify man's experience, which he seeks, but he cannot verify the metaphysical reality of these ideas.[11] Another issue faces these ideas in that since there is no physical experience of them, one cannot even be sure if the normal structures of causality, space, or time applies to them. There is simply not a lot that can be known about them.[12] They are, for Kant, "antinomies," in that he believes that one could argue equally for their existence or non-existence.[13]

These transcendental antinomies may seem familiar as they are essentially the fundamental realities that make up man's worldview. The antinomies include the metaphysical identity in things, as well as man's origin, identity, and purpose. Kant's philosophy convinced those of the time that these metaphysical realities were beyond the reach of human reason, hence ushering in a wave of anti-rational skepticism. Likewise,

---

[11] Ibid., 311. "The function of these ideas is simply and solely regulative. As regulative ideas they give us a reasonable way of dealing with the constantly recurring questions raised by metaphysics."

[12] Ibid., 312.

[13] Ibid., 313.

another philosophical aftermath of Kant's Critical philosophy is that philosophy becomes e-quated with epistemology. The physical sciences continue to grow, but the traditional metaphysical pursuits that characterized the central question of the history of philosophy, *"What is it?"*, are dropped for a period.[14] In the wake of the collapse of the Metaphysical Theistic worldview, a perfect setting is created in which a new worldview of Methodological Naturalism could arise.

Methodological Naturalism as Worldview

As was mentioned previously, in the 19th century the physical sciences hit a period of exponential growth. At the same time it had this success, there was a corresponding worldview shift of those practicing science towards Methodological Naturalism. An underlying premise of this worldview was that all physical phenomena could be explained by reference to material causes, not the immaterial identity which was traditionally held to stand at the root of a thing's being. Kant, again, had shown such realities to be unknowable. The

---

[14] Ortega y Gasset, *What is Philosophy?*, 46.

universe could, therefore, only be an infinite closed system of matter and energy in which everything could be explained in reference to itself. A system must exist that had no need for God in any explanatory fashion.[15] In the field of physics, Pierre Laplace attempted to explain the formation of the solar system through references only to material causes, like gravity.[16] In the field of geology, scientist Charles Lyell believed he could explain the development of all the physical features of the earth by reference to long swaths of time combined with natural processes. In biology, Darwin challenged the traditional theistic design arguments by claiming to explain the origin and development of living species from the processes of natural selection and random mutation. The overall conclusion of the combination of Rationalist metaphysical skepticism with these scientific advances created, what has been called, the "seamless garment of naturalism."[17] In their eyes,

---

[15] Stephen Meyer, "The Return of the God Hypothesis." *Journal of Interdisciplinary Studies*, no. 11 (1999), 168.

[16] Ibid., 167.

[17] Ibid., 168. "These theories taken jointly suggested that the whole history of the universe could be

man's history was no longer one tied up with the transcendent, but instead with a history of accidental causes flowing from an ultimately meaningless non-conscious source. Given such a radical change, this new story of Methodological Naturalism was bound to shape man's identity and purpose in the same vein.

Charles Darwin knew this to be true, as he did not stop his writing with the famous *Origin of Species*. He continued its application to the realm of human beings and culture with his work *The Descent of Man*.[18] The heart of Darwin's claim is

---

told as a seamless, or nearly seamless, unfolding of the potentiality of matter and energy. Thus, science seemed to support, if it could be said to support anything, a materialistic or naturalistic worldview, not a theistic one. Science no longer needed to invoke a pre-existent mind to shape matter in order to explain the evidence of nature. Matter had always existed and could - in effect - arrange itself without a pre-existent designer or Creator."

[18] *Human Zoos, America's Forgotten History of Scientific Racism*. Directed by John G. West. (Seattle, WA: Discovery Institute, 2018.) Even though Social Darwinism is considered a taboo subject today, it is not clear what has changed within the Naturalist worldview to make it so, other than the fact that its practical applications have been deemed unpalatable.

that man is fundamentally an animal. This is in contradistinction to the Metaphysical Theistic view that man is body and soul, that his immaterial form has been created by God and will be called back to God with the death of the body. Darwin is aware of the traditional philosophical arguments for the immaterial soul, but he recognizes that if man is qualitatively different from the animals then evolution could not be an adequate explanation of man's origin.[19] [20] Darwin's response is an insistence that there is in reality no qualitative difference, only a quantitative one.

The early formulators of Naturalism were not as shy in embracing the logical conclusions of their ideas. Many have not heard of the "human zoos" in the United States where Africans were imported and put on display as the missing link in the evolutionary chain, but they happened.

[19] Charles Darwin, *The Descent of Man* (London: Penguin Books, 2004), 38.

[20] Ibid., 43. "It has been asserted that man alone is capable of progressive improvement … that no animal has the power of abstraction, or of forming general concepts, is self-conscious and comprehends itself; that no animal employs language; that man alone has a sense of beauty, is liable to caprice, has the feeling of gratitude, mystery; believes in God, or is endowed with a conscience."

Man and animals are really the same; they just exist on a scale of quantitative growth.[21] Darwin tries to validate his claim throughout the book by finding similarities between animals and men based on common biology. He then extrapolates out the similarities using equivocal words to make it look as though there is a real connection. He repeats this formula over and over, but through all his attempts he never really addresses the qualitative differences that would get at the heart of the matter. Macroscopic changes are not explained but are just assumed as extrapolations of the microscopic relations. While it can be argued whether or not Darwin successfully proved his argument, that is his claim.

---

[21] Ibid., 43. "If no organic being excepting man had possessed any mental power, or if his powers had been of a wholly different nature from those of the lower animals, then we should never have been able to convince ourselves that our high faculties had been gradually developed. But it can be shewn that there is no fundamental difference of this kind. We must also admit that there is a much wider interval in mental power between one of the lowest fishes, as a lamprey or lancelet, and one of the higher apes, than between an ape and man; *yet this interval is filled up by numberless generations.*"

The implications for those who accept his argument are just as important, as they entail the destruction of teleological morality because man no longer *has* a nature. Rather, man *is* nature, and nature cares solely about the survival of the fittest. The ultimate and sole arbiter of action is survival. Now this might mean, as Darwin argues, that humans must work together to survive and therefore care about one another enough to develop a social morality.[22] But it could just as easily mean the opposite. He uses the example of bees who kill their family members. If they too developed enough to share in the ability to reason, he argues that their morality would still be to kill one another, indeed, their duty to do so. Ultimately, Darwin sees morality as the inbred biological instinct that is born from the necessary workings of survival.[23]

---

[22] Ibid., 55.

[23] Ibid., 52. "If, for instance, to take an extreme case, men were reared under precisely the same conditions as hive-bees, there can hardly be a doubt that our unmarried females would, like the worker-bees, think it a sacred duty to kill their brothers, and mothers would strive to kill their fertile daughters; and no one would think of interfering."

On a social level, Darwin's conclusion is that morality is ultimately based in a type of social utilitarianism within the fight for survival and reproduction. It is the good of the community that is important, not necessarily the individual. As evidence of this, Darwin makes the point that in primitive tribes there is an ethic that is shared among the community that is in no way transferred to individuals outside the tribe.[24] Darwin also seemingly laments the lack of natural selection that takes place within human societies.[25] Thomas Huxley, one of Darwin's greatest proponents in the 19th century, put it plainly when he talks about how there is no reason to favor the evolution of the traditionally "moral" sentiments over the "immoral." Both are products of evolution according to Huxley.[26] Dostoyevsky, too, saw

---

[24] Ibid., 59.

[25] Ibid., 65. "We civilized men, on the other hand, do our utmost to check the process of elimination … Thus the weak members of civilized societies propagate their kind. No one who has attended to the breeding of domestic animals will doubt that this must be highly injurious to the race of man."

[26] Thomas Huxley, *Evolution and Ethics* (Fairfield, IA: 1st World Library, 2003), 75. "... the immoral sentiments have no less been evolved, there is, so far, as

the implications of this way of viewing morality in his work *Crime and Punishment*. He places in the mouth of a group of young people the new ethics of the time as they lament the existence of a horrible old pawnbroker who offers nothing to society except the hoarding of her money. They speculate about the hundreds or thousands of people they could help by just killing her. "One death, and a hundred lives in exchange—it's simple arithmetic!" they say. They compare her to a bug, saying that nature could not produce great men unless such abominations as this woman are eliminated. Thus, it is their duty to aid nature in her natural process of the survival of the fittest.[27]

---

much natural sanction for the one as the other. The thief and the murderer follow nature just as much as the philanthropist. … it is incompetent to furnish any better reason why what we call good is preferable to what we call evil than we had before."

[27] Fyodor Dostoyevsky, *Crime and Punishment* (New York: Vintage Books, 1950), 58-61. "Besides, what value has the life of that sickly, stupid, ill-natured old woman in the balance of existence! No more than the life of a louse, of a black-beetle, less in fact because the old woman is doing harm. She is wearing out the lives of others; … "Of course she does not deserve to live," remarked the officer, "but there it is, it's nature."

It seems hard to overstate the universal influence that Darwin's ideas had on the world at the time and continues to have on the numberless academics who begin their work from the premises of Methodological Naturalism. All their experimental data and conclusions are formulated by the tenets of naturalism. Alternate explanations of data that are not produced within those tenets are often viewed as simply absurd. One philosopher who expressly laid out the implications of Darwin's ideas on the philosophical world of the 20th century was John Dewey. Dewey is included in this thesis because he represents that popular trend of naturalism still present in today's society to accept only the validity of the physical sciences. In his work *The Influence of Darwin on Philosophy and Other Essays,* Dewey is so convinced by Darwin's work that he is willing to say that the *Origin of Species* fundamentally changed the nature of the history of philosophy.

"Oh, well, brother, but we have to correct and direct nature, and, but for that, we should drown in an ocean of prejudice. But for that, there would never have been a single great man."

Dewey makes the claim that Darwin destroyed the idea of the formal reality in things. It was the immaterial substantial forms which had reigned since the Greeks, giving a thing its fixed nature and telos.[28] Man had forever been searching for the identity in things which transcended the varied flux of daily life and change. He ventured to seek such an identity in the transcendent and immaterial before being willing to consider such identity in the realm of the physical. To break the idea of species in the realm of the philosophy of nature and metaphysics was to open the floodgates to new ideas in the rest of society as well.[29] To do away with metaphysical essences, Dewey notes, is to have a drastic impact on logic, religion, politics, and morality. It is to precipitate a worldview crisis of sorts.[30]

This is not a crisis that Dewey is worried about, though. Actually, he expresses a sense of

---

[28] John Dewey, *The Influence of Darwin on Philosophy and Other Essays* (New York: Henry Holt and Company, 1910), at A John Dewey Source Page, www.brocku.ca/MeadProject/
Dewey/Dewey_1910b/Dewey_1910)01.html. ch I pt I.

[29] Ibid., ch I pt II.

[30] Ibid., ch I pt I.

optimism because man no longer is searching for ultimate answers. He is no longer trying to find a transcendent solution to man's daily problems. He has removed his gaze from the afterlife in order to focus it here on this life. In doing so he has the ability to make this life better for all around him. Dewey sees no use for philosophical abstractions since they are not real. Why talk about essences if no such essences exist? Dewey wants to learn about the physical world, rather than rely on God for explanations, or speak in the terms of outmoded philosophy. In fact, science does not even bother itself anymore with trying to refute philosophy. Rather, it must simply just abandon philosophical questions altogether.[31]

----

[31] Ibid., ch I pt IV. "Old ideas give way slowly; for they are more than abstract logical forms and categories. They are habits, predispositions, deeply engrained attitudes of aversion and preference. Moreover, the conviction persists-though history shows it to be a hallucination that all the questions that the human mind has asked are questions that can be answered in terms of the alternatives that the questions themselves present. But in fact intellectual progress usually occurs through sheer abandonment of questions together with both of the alternatives they assume an abandonment that results from their decreasing vitality and a

Dewey addresses this discussion in some depth in his work *Experience and Nature*. There, he makes the argument that religion and philosophy were modes of thinking developed to answer questions relevant to the past. Man faced an onslaught of difficulties in his short fight for survival like famine, disease, natural disaster, war, and death. These resulted in a constant desire for some type of overarching narrative to make sense of it all.[32] The questions were never fully answered, though, and persisted over the centuries even as the times and circumstances of human society changed and the questions became outmoded. At a certain point, if the questions are not relevant anymore, the whole mode of searching for answers to them must change as well. The

---

change of urgent interest. We do not solve them: we get over them. Old questions are solved by disappearing, evaporating, while new questions corresponding to the changed attitude of endeavor and preference take their place. Doubtless the greatest dissolvent in contemporary thought of old questions, the greatest precipitant of new methods, new intentions, new problems, is the one effected by the scientific revolution that found its climax in the "Origin of Species."

[32] John Dewey, *Experience and Nature* (Mccutchen Press, 2011), Kindle. 54.

great perennial questions are not defeated, they are just abandoned. If this fails to happen, then society is stuck searching for an answer that does not exist. Even worse, for Dewey, these questions can be subverted to get people to think about the afterlife instead of this life.[33]

In place of philosophy, Dewey proposes his method of "empirical naturalism." This worldview incorporates the premises of naturalism as it does not try to refute perennial philosophy. It considers itself successful if it can give a materialist explanation for the existence of such questions, and therefore simply dismiss them.[34] It is also empirical in that it is the application of the scientific method to all aspects of society in the place of philosophy. Dewey's faith in the scientific method is based on the fact that science is able to shift and change itself based on new discoveries. It is not tied down to any particular position or idea. It is simply the process of development of ideas. It poses a question that can be answered, a process by which to answer it, and a mechanism

---

[33] Ibid., 56, 61-3.
[34] Ibid., 66.

by which to admit it was wrong and update it-self.[35]

The method of empirical naturalism is to be applied even to the realm of human morality and value. In Dewey's work *The Quest for Certainty*, he admits that providing a theory of moral value within empirical naturalism is one of his greatest problems.[36] Nevertheless, at the end of *Experience and Nature*, he tries to do just that. Again, as met-aphysical essences have been rejected, so too is the traditional moral structure of teleological end. Dewey argues that things have many varied ends, as reality itself consists of an ever changing flux. All that Dewey can recognize in his new worldview is that man experiences positive or negative values, but nothing much more can be said.[37] There are those who try to create systems,

_____

[35] Ibid., 57, 66.

[36] John Dewey, *Quest For Certainty* of *Twentieth-Century Philosophy* (Upper Saddle River, NJ: Prentice Hall, 2003), 27.

[37] Dewey, *Experience and Nature*, 474-478. "It must surrender the identification of natural ends with good and perfection; recognizing that a natural end, apart from endeavor expressing choice, has no intrin-sic eulogistic quality … death, ignorance, as well as life, are finalities."

or criticisms, of value and turn it into something abstract.[38] To incorporate values into some type of worldview narrative is not possible for Dewey, as this is what philosophy tried to do in the past. There can only be a simpler discrimination between values in daily life to ensure that positive value does not cease.[39] If one must deny themselves some pleasure in the immediate, it is only to enjoy a more refined pleasure in the next moment. There are no higher-order laws governing this process, only the desire to experience positive value as one desires. Delayed gratification is not inherently more moral than immediate gratification; they are just as different as the immediate sugar rush of a soda versus the refined taste of an aged wine.[40]

If there is an attempt to incorporate the immediate experience of value into a larger worldview narrative, one must recognize that those

---

[38] Ibid., 474-8.

[39] Ibid., 478-85. If one eats cookies before their dinner then the positive experience of the satiation of hunger at dinner is lost, thus one could discriminate and say to eat cookies after dinner.

[40] Ibid., 478-85.

fundamental beliefs about the world are themselves values for Dewey. Those beliefs are a choice
one makes about how to look at things, not reflec-
tions about the structure of the world. And as
Dewey already mentioned, many of these religious and philosophical worldviews are outdated,
incompatible with the modern world. All must be
subjected to the physical verification of the scientific method. Scientific verification is the only objective value.[41] If philosophy has any role at all, it
is to help bring about the implications of the scientific method into the language of all disci-
plines.[42] Dewey also argues that the old philosophical and religious systems should not limit
man's conception of himself. The old structures
in society which reflect these old narratives need
to be torn down, allowing man to broaden the
vista of his experience.

Besides valuing the scientific method itself,
Dewey does make the claim that art and social
companionship are self-evident values as well,[43]
though it seems unclear how science is able to

---

[41] Ibid., 490.
[42] Ibid., 485-92.
[43] Ibid., 492-9.

make such claims regarding complex values. 20th century philosopher F. C. Copleston makes the point that Dewey's system of values cannot really speak about much more than what is positive for the biological growth of the body. Any claim beyond that is unfounded.[44] If Dewey cannot come up with a coherent theory of moral value, there is still nothing to fear in his mind, because implicit in empirical naturalism is that some day science will make sense out of it. More time and experiments are needed.[45]

---

[44] Frederick Copleston, *A History of Philosophy Volume VIII: Modern Philosophy Empiricism, Idealism, and Pragmatism in Britain and America* (New York: Doubleday, 1994), 369/370. "Indeed, 'growth itself is the only moral 'end'. Again, 'growing, or the continuous reconstruction of experience, is the only end.' A natural question to ask is, growth in what direction? Reconstruction for what purpose? But if such questions concern a final end other than growth itself, reconstruction itself, they can have no meaning in terms of Dewey's philosophy. He does indeed admit that happiness or the satisfaction of the forces of human nature is the moral end. But as happiness turns out to be living, while 'life means growth', we seem to be back at the same point."

[45] Dewey, *Quest For Certainty*, 27.

Nihilism As Worldview

The failure of science to provide a system of moral values is also a central theme in the worldview of Nihilism and in the philosophy of Friedrich Nietzsche. In chapter one, it was mentioned that worldviews possess people, whether for good or bad. They transcend the individual to such an extent that when an individual adopts them, they become an incarnation of those ideas. Very few men have seemed to be more possessed by their ideas than someone like Friedrich Nietzsche.[46] A biographer, James Miller, recounts that when Nietzsche was an early teen studying the literature and philosophy of Ancient Greece he, like Socrates, called out for the inspiration of a daimon to guide him. "I want to know thee, O unknown power, That thrusts its hand into my soul, Raging through my life like a storm, O unfathomable One, my kinsman! I want to know thee and serve thee." Nietzsche's plea was answered. In his college journals, he reveals a mind that was seemingly guided by the inspirations of

---

[46] James Miller, *Examined Lives: From Socrates to Nietzsche* (New York: Picador, 2012), 321.

the demonic.[47] A book that he was guided to buy
was by the 19th-century atheist Arthur Schopenhauer, a figure who would be deeply influential to
Nietzsche.[48] In Schopenhauer's work he would
find the "... deification and transformation of the
very heart of mankind."[49]

This radical transformation of the heart of
mankind would begin from the loss of the key-
stone in the arch of Western ideas, the death of
God, from which everything else would tumble
down into meaningless chaos. Why is God dead?
Kant had destroyed man's ability to know metaphysical reality.[50] Darwin, likewise, banished the

---

[47] Ibid., 319-21. "...his journals and notebooks tell
the story of a tormented young man who was frequently ill and subject to hallucinatory visions. "What
I fear," he wrote in one journal entry, "is not the fearful
character behind my chair,' apparently referring to his
daimon, "but his voice: and not his words, but the ter-
rifying inarticulate and inhuman tone of this character. If only it spoke as humans speak!" ... While brows-
ing a secondhand bookshop, "I saw this book," he re-
called in an autobiographical essay, and "I took it
down and began to turn the pages. Then a demon
whispered in my ear: 'Take this book home with you.'"

[48] Ibid., 321.

[49] Ibid., 322.

[50] De Lubac. *The Drama of Atheist Humanism*, 46.

metaphysical from the realm of nature. What then is there to know? There is nothing left to know. There never was anything to know. God has been a projection, a tool of power in a historical struggle.[51] Kant, with his Critical Epistemology, has provided man with the keys to his own jail cell, the jail cell of Christianity. Man, though, must choose to free himself from his bondage by an act of the will, by banishing God once for all from the human mind.[52] Nietzsche, then, is the harbinger of this liberation who calls humanity to take the key and free itself.[53] The death of God is at the same time the birth of the worldview of Nihilism, as it is the death of all objective values. Nietzsche, then, has also come to proclaim the implications for mankind in the death of all former values. Like a tsunami following an earthquake, Nietzsche proclaimed the rise of a black

---

[51] Ibid., 44.

[52] Ibid., 46. "For the rest, his [Kant] criticism was bound to be incomplete because it remained wholly speculative and did not proceed from a decision. Kant was only an intellectual, a 'journeyman of philosophy': it is man who has to free himself, by an act of will. He must dare."

[53] Ibid., 46.

wave of Nihilism which would follow the earth-shattering death of God.[54]

Before man can really understand what is involved in the death of objective values, Nietzsche argues that one must understand historically why such a term even exists. Man must reconfigure his notion of history. In many ways, Nietzsche's retelling of history corresponds to Darwin's account as he says that there has been an implicit class structure that has always existed in all societies.[55] It is a biological fact that there is always an inherent struggle for power. The "will to life" is

---

[54] Ibid., 64-5 footnote. "I herald the coming of a tragic era ... We must be prepared for a long succession of demolitions, devastations, and upheavals ... there will be wars such as the world has never yet seen ... Europe will soon be enveloped in darkness ... we shall watch the rising of a black tide ... Our whole European civilization is in a state of anguished anticipation; it is making its way, decade by decade, toward catastrophe with a restless, irresistible movement, increasingly hastened by a river that runs to its end, that no longer reflects, that would be afraid to reflect."

[55] Friedrich Nietzsche. *Beyond Good and Evil.* of *Philosophy: A Historical Survey With Essential Readings 10th Edition.* (New York: McGraw Hill Education, 2020), 332.

that there be a "will to power" among creatures.[56] Historically, Nietzsche claims that this struggle split humanity into two fundamental groups, "master" and "slave," the "higher man" and the "lower man."[57] As such, universal morality is not possible.[58] What's the distinction between master and slave morality? Nietzsche says that universally the master morality has always been the morality of the physically powerful and dominant. The strong take control of society and determine morality as they see fit. They create morality. The slave has always been physically weak, subject to his master. The slave tries to gain the upper hand by inverting morality, turning it from an entity of power to an abstract and rational entity. The slave pushes virtue, generosity, kindness, and the good of the whole in order to preserve the weak bodies

---

[56] Ibid., 333.

[57] Ibid., 332.

[58] Ibid., 332. "'Exploitation' does not belong to a depraved, or imperfect and primitive society: it belongs to the nature of the living being as a primary organic function; it is a consequence of the intrinsic Will to Power, which is precisely the Will to Life. - Granting that as a theory this is a novelty - as a reality it is the fundamental fact of all history: let us be so far honest towards ourselves!"

of slaves from exploitation.[59] The slave morality is the "... morality which sees precisely in sympathy, or in acting for the good of others, or in self-disinterest, the characteristic of moral...".[60]

Having a new history, a godless struggle for power between the strong and weak, man can now consider what it even means to experience "value." Nietzsche probes the question about value almost as far as it can go. He asks why Western society has valued the idea of "truth" at all. Who commanded that this was a value? Why was elevating the philosophical search for the identity in things the right choice to make? There is something more fundamental than truth as a value, and that is will. Is it not the will of man that decided that truth should be valued? Why should man not will the opposite?[61] One might object

---

[59] Ibid., 334-5.

[60] Ibid., 334.

[61] Ibid., 1. "Just who is it anyway who has been asking these questions? Just what is it in us that wants 'to approach truth'? Indeed, we tarried a long time before the question of the cause of this will [to search for truth]. And in the end we stopped altogether before the even more basic question. We asked 'What is the value of this will?' Supposing we want truth: why not rather untruth? Uncertainty? Even ignorance?"

that logical and abstract truths, universal principles, first causes, and immaterial forms all corre-
spond to the nature of reality. Here, Nietzsche in-
vokes the same death-knell as Kant, Darwin, and
(later on) Dewey. He rejects the idea that reality
is anything more than the physical appearance of
things. This idea of "things-in-themselves" was
made up. It was an idea that was weaponized by
the slave class to tame the master class.[62]

Nietzsche pins part of the blame on the supposedly degenerate historical figure of Socrates.
Socrates changed philosophy to be something abstract, a discipline where its highest answers were
in the intellectual realm instead of the physical.[63]

---

[62] Ibid., 2. "Their basis must lie in the womb of Being, in the Eternal, in the hidden God, in the 'Thing In
Itself' - here, and nowhere else! - This type of judgment
is the typical prejudice by which the metaphysicians of
all time can be recognized. This type of valuation
stands back of all their logical methods; this is the
'faith' that enables them to struggle for what they call
'knowing' - a something which at last they solemnly
christen 'truth.' The basic faith of all metaphysicians is
faith in the antithetical nature of values."

[63] Friedrich Nietzsche. *Twilight of the Idols.* Series
Five Book 24 of *Delphi Complete Works of Friedrich*

Reality, for Nietzsche, exists in Heraclitus' notion of flux. Instead of seeking to exit Plato's cave, man must return to the cave wall where the shadows of the empirical, physical, and changing exist.[64] In so many words, Nietzsche fundamentally rejects the existence of the metaphysical realm. Instead, man has used such concepts to create God and keep him alive by religious ritual.[65]

> "Thus they arrive at their stupendous concept, "God" That which is last, thinnest, and emptiest is put first, as the cause, as *ens realissimum*. Why did mankind have to take seriously the brain afflictions of sick web-spinners?"[66]

If metaphysical truths, like God and immaterial essences, are the reversal of physical and bodily values that nature endowed humans with, then really at the core of value is something like deception. The slave class are deceivers seeking power

---

Nietzsche. (United Kingdom: Delphi Classics, 2015), 3045, 3061.

[64] Ibid., 3060.
[65] Ibid., 3061.
[66] Ibid.

and control.[67] In doing this, Nietzsche is redefining the fundamental values of the Western
worldview. Respect for truth, delayed gratification, universal human dignity, and the like are
ideas which only make sense if one favors the
metaphysical interpretation of reality. Those like
Socrates have claimed that metaphysical truth
was most fundamentally self-evident, but Nietzsche rejects this.[68] This is also to reject any sem-
blance of logic. To assert that something is logi-
cally true or untrue is to implicitly assent to the
metaphysical worldview. Nietzsche says that
those who challenge this interpretation of reality
hold dear those very claims which are illogical.
Here one can see what it means to be "beyond
good and evil," as there is no longer any system
by which to adjudicate any interpretation of reality on a rational level. All that exists are feelings,

---

[67] Nietzsche. *Beyond Good and Evil,* 3.

[68] Ibid., 3. "Even behind logic and its apparent sov-
ereignty of development stand values judgments, or, to
speak more plainly, physiological demands for pre-
serving a certain type of life. Such as for example, that
the definite is worth more than the indefinite, that appearance is less valuable than 'the truth.'"

urges, instincts, and power.[69] To be beyond good
and evil is to enter the realm of Nihilism. It is to
enter a worldview which denies all worldviews
except those that the powerful choose to assert on
their subjects. Science, likewise, is simply a tool
without value in the biased hands of the philosopher. He may do with it what he sees fit.[70]

Now that man understands his history, he
understands himself, and there is but one part of
Nietzsche's nihilistic worldview to fill in, namely
his purpose. If the metaphysicians of the past expressed their "metaphysics of projection" by creating rational connections in reality where there
were actually none,[71] then they have unduly controlled the narrative of society.[72] What must happen, then, is that Nihilism must destroy this control and return man back to his primordial state

---

[69] Ibid., 4.

[70] Ibid., 7. "... there is nothing impersonal whatever
in the philosopher. And particularly his morality testi-
fies decidedly and decisively as to who he is-that is,
what order of rank the innermost desires of his nature
occupy."

[71] Nietzsche, *Twilight of the Idols*, 3077.

[72] Ibid., 3089.

of the Dionysian. This is most importantly repre-
sented in the work of overthrowing Christianity.
Christianity spiritualized certain "good" parts of
man's being. Now man must begin to accept even
the darkest parts of his being as just as valuable as
the lighter parts.[73]

Communism As Worldview

Finally, we will consider the worldview of
Communism. One will notice that there are many
similarities among these materialist worldviews,
though Marx approaches his conclusions from a
slightly different angle. Marx was deeply influ-
enced by Hegel's notions of historical dialectic
and the absolute spirit. He was not interested,
though, in continuing a conservative strand of
Hegelianism but bringing it into the light of new
historical circumstances,[74] crediting the insights

---

[73] Ibid., 3076, 3079, 3080.

[74] Karl Marx, "Critique of the Hegelian Dialectic
and Philosophy as a Whole." In *Economic and Philosophic Manuscripts of* 1844: Prep. Institute of Marxism-Leninism (Moscow: Foreign Languages Publishing House, 1956), 142-3.

of Ludwig Feuerbach for helping him.[75] Feuerbach and Marx claim that Hegel erred in accepting that the most real part of reality as the immaterial, abstract, and absolute instead of the physical, changing, and material. In doing so, Hegel
could not fully realize the consequences of the
materialist revolution.[76] Rather, he has actually
estranged man from himself because he has convinced himself that what is most real is that which
is least tied to the material world. The traditional
philosopher is likewise an alienated man bringing

---

[75] Marx, "Critique of the Hegelian Dialectic and
Philosophy as a Whole," 145. "Feuerbach's great
achievement is: (1) The proof that philosophy is nothing else but religion rendered into thoughts and think-
ingly expounded, and that is has likewise to be con-
demned as an other form and manner of existence of
the estrangement of the essence of man; (2) The estab-
lishment of true materialism and or real science, since
Feuerbach also makes the social relationship 'of man
to man' the basic principle of the theory; (3) His opposing to the negation of the negation, which claims to
be the absolute positive, the self-supporting positive,
positively grounded on itself."

[76] Ibid., 145-6.

about estrangement of human beings from material reality.[77] Hegel negated his negation of metaphysics by reestablishing it in the synthesis phase
of his dialectic. If Materialism is just a phase of
man's developing psyche, which is really a deeper
and deeper connection into the immaterial world,
then ultimately even Materialism will be brought
into a type of Spiritualism again as the human
mind proceeds towards its own deification in the
absolute spirit.[78]

Marx does not accept the synthesis phase of
Hegel's reasoning; rather, he concludes that Hegel has really shown the metaphysical realm of

---

[77] Ibid., 147-9.

[78] Ibid., 150-3. "But it is equally clear that a self-
consciousness- can only establish thing hood through
its alienation - i.e. establish something which itself is
only an abstract thing, a thing of abstraction and not a
real thing. It is clear, further, that thing hood is therefore utterly without any independence, any essentiality
vis-à-vis self-consciousness; that on the contrary it is a
mere creature - something posited by self-consciousness. And what is posited, instead of confirming itself,
is but a confirmation of the act of positing in which is
concentrated for a moment the energy of the act as its
product, seeming to give the deposit-but only for a
moment- the character of an independent, real substance."

immaterial essences, God, and the soul to be simply projections of man's mind. Man projects the existence of the spiritual world, giving it importance in society and bringing about alienation from his true self.[79] Therefore, religion is the worst of all illusions as it causes man to sacrifice the present for an afterlife that does not exist.

If I know religion as alienated human self-consciousness then what I know in it as religion is not my self-consciousness but my *alienated* self-consciousness confirmed in it. I know my own self, the self-consciousness that belongs to its very nature, therefore, confirmed not in religion but in annihilated and superseded religion.[80]

There are also structures in society which reflect this delusion and alienation. Marx lists some, including "private rights, morality, the family, civil society, and the state." The faster that man can realize these ideas and institutions are fake, the sooner a true humanism can take place where there will be no forms of alienation. With religion gone, and the social sphere equalized through

---

[79] Ibid., 158, 160.
[80] Ibid., 161.

Communism, man can truly be free.[81] As long as it remains, "His [man's] thoughts are therefore fixed mental shapes or ghosts dwelling outside nature and man."[82] De Lubac describes their conception of God as a vampiric figure who sucks the life blood from human beings for himself. He's the hidden man behind the curtain that has controlled the lives of too many people. This vampiric figure must be exorcized, and the curtain must be torn down. Only then can man see that there was nothing behind the curtain except a mirror; it was all a projection of man's psyche.[83] [84]

---

[81] Ibid., 161-64.

[82] Ibid., 168.

[83] De Lubac. *The Drama of Atheist Humanism*, 44.

[84] Cardinal Robert Sarah and Nicholas Diat, *The Day is Now Far Spent* (Ignatius Press. San Francisco, 2019), 239-40. This quote is from an article by Aleksandr Solzhenitsyn in 1985 in *Le Figaro*. "The world had never before known a godlessness as organized, militarized, and tenaciously malevolent as that practiced by Marxism. Within the philosophical system of Marx and Lenin, and at the heart of their psychology, hatred of God is the principal driving force, more fundamental than all their political and economic pretensions. Militant atheism is not merely incidental or marginal to Communist polity, it is not a side effect,

The Kingdom of God, then, has been transformed into the unlimited potential of the "Kingdom of Man." Man, not God, is the measure of all
things. The question becomes, how does one get
people to hear and accept the truth of this mes-
sage? It involves getting people to wake up from
their opiate-induced sleep brought about by their
focusing on the afterlife. It is like a chain covered

---

but the central pivot. The 1920's in the USSR witnessed
an uninterrupted procession of victims and martyrs
whom, Veniamin of Petrograd, had been elected by the
popular vote of his diocese. Patriarch Tikhon himself
passed through the hands of the Cheka-GPU and then
died under suspicious circumstances. Scores of arch-
bishops and bishops perished. Tens of thousands of
priests, monks, and nuns, pressured by the Chekists to
renounce the Word of God, were tortured, shot in cel-
lars, sent to camps, exiled to the desolate tundra of the
far North, or turned out into the streets in their old age
without food or shelter. All these Christian martyrs
went unswervingly to their deaths for the faith; in-
stances of apostasy were few and far between. For tens
of millions of laymen access to the Church was
blocked, and they were forbidden to bring up their
children in the Faith: religious parents were wrenched
from their children and thrown into prison, while the
children were turned from the faith by threats and
lies."

by flowers which is draped over someone's shoulders. Even if it looks pretty, it weighs them down into immobility.[85] Practical action is necessary. More specifically, a revolution which grasps at the roots of society and transforms them is necessary. Anything that reflects man's old alienation must go.[86] One of the key necessary ingredients in this revolution is the creation of a clear group structure of "oppressor" and "oppressed." In doing this, the good people of the movement can be clearly distinguished from its enemies. Likewise, once things have been organized into this duality, it will become clear that the old structure of society cannot fully address the historical problem of oppression. The collapse of the whole of the old

---

[85] Karl Marx, "Critique of Hegel's Philosophy of Right." In *Karl Marx: Early Writings*. Trans. and Ed. by T.B. Bottomore. (New York: McGraw Hill, 1963), 43-4.

[86] Ibid., 52. "What proves beyond doubt the radicalism of Germany theory, and thus its practical energy, is that it begins from the resolute positive abolition of religion. The criticism of religion ends with the doctrine that man is the supreme being for man. It ends, therefore, with the categorical imperative to overthrow all those conditions in which man is abased, enslaved, abandoned, contemptible being …"

society is needed in order to create a new one.[87] Having the ability to socially engineer society through continued revolutionary action, the utopia can be brought into being for humanity.[88] Truth, for Marx, is nothing other than what the powerful has proclaimed it to be.[89] There is no human nature, just how humans have been arranged into groups by society.[90] In the end, Communism aspired to be "a binding doctrine, comprehensive teaching, an all-embracing Weltanschauung."[91]

In conclusion, it is clear that the catastrophes of the 20th century can now be explained by reference to how these new worldviews crafted reality

---

[87] Ibid., 58. "For one class to be the liberating class par excellence, it is necessary that another class should be openly the oppressing class. The negative significance of the French nobility and clergy produced the positive significance of the bourgeoisie…"

[88] Karl Marx, "Theses on Feuerbach." In *Economic and Philosophic Manuscripts of 1844*. Prep. Institute of Marxism-Leninism (Moscow: Foreign Languages Publishing House, 1956), 244-5.

[89] Ibid., 243.

[90] Ibid., 245.

[91] Hans Kung. *Does God Exist? An Answer For Today* (New York: Doubleday & Company, 1980), 237.

in their image through a radical destruction of the existing theistic structures in society. This action does not happen without consequences, though. How does one force a population to submit to a new grand narrative to which they do not assent? The answer is Arendt's answer, through coercion and manipulation of a population in every form and manner.

While these philosophies may have denied the existence of the immaterial identity in things through force, that did not magically make the metaphysical side of reality disappear. People are inherently ordered toward the transcendent. To try to destroy this impulse, according to Dosto-yevsky, requires a mountain of severed heads.[92] Even in the face of a mountain built by severed heads (as was seen in the 20th century), like plants paved over by concrete, the metaphysical will always find a way to spring back up into human life. They are the perennial questions, after all, and

---

[92] Dostoyevsky, *The Possessed*, 450. "They shout 'a hundred million heads'; that may be only a metaphor; but why be afraid of it if, with the slow day-dream on paper, despotism in the course of some hundred years will devour not a hundred but five hundred million heads?"

though Dewey may choose to abandon them, they will continue to grow into a regenerated forest waiting to be found by the next generation. This is Arendt's concluding hope at the end of *The Origins of Totalitarianism*, that the birth of a new generation would provide a fresh view of reality which would be free from ideological manipulation.[93]

---

[93] Arendt, *The Origins of Totalitarianism*, 478-9.

Chapter III

The Perennial Return
of Metaphysical Theism

The Incompleteness of Scientism

Jose Ortega y Gasset begins his work *What is Philosophy?* by affirming this very claim—that even if the metaphysical side of existence is suppressed, it will always return to man's consciousness. Gasset mentions that, beginning in the 1800's, a form of scientism had convinced many people that philosophy would be replaced. But even by the 1920's, he points out that there was again a longing in people's consciousness for answers that science could not provide. Physics, with all its enticing innovations, had shown itself incomplete as a substitute for philosophy.[1] It had addicted the Western world with bodily comforts

---

[1] Ortega y Gasset, *What is Philosophy?*, 16.

and pleasures, but this was not necessarily a virtue. The "imperialism of physics" had attempted
to convince society that truth was reducible to scientific utility. While someone like Dewey would
agree, saying that philosophical questions are
"unanswerable" and should be abandoned, Gasset insists that science cannot bring about fulfillment for the human condition. When science is
exalted as the ultimate arbiter of truth, all that
happens is that the uniquely human realm in society becomes subjugated to an inadequate master.[2] He adds, "the intellectual life of Europe has
for almost a hundred years suffered from what
one might call the 'terrorism of the laborato-
ries.'"[3] After all, the 19th and 20th centuries were
times of massive change and upheaval, so it is not
surprising for men to cling onto that which is
practical and most clear to the human disposition
of knowing. But it was not adequate.

One of the themes of Gasset's work was the
idea of worldview "crisis." When the structures of
society change so rapidly that the different coex-

---

[2] Ibid., 41-6.
[3] Ibid., 46.

isting generations cannot understand one another, or feel alienated from one another, there is going to be a serious collapse and imminent crisis. He even mentions that he would scare people if he divulged all he saw coming toward Western man in the 20th century.[4] It is in the face of this complexity, though, where the philosophical conversation, as such, is continually reborn.

Man's Original Disorientation

Gasset's starting point of philosophy is that man's life is fundamentally fragmented as a set of individual experiences and situations. Such a life of disparate unconnected moments is not palatable for human beings, though. In such a state a disorienting effect is produced. In fact, Gasset claims that man's most basic state is complete dis-

---

[4] Ibid., 38.

"The change is going to be far more radical than what we are now seeing, and it will penetrate so far down through the various deep strata of human life that, taught by past experience, I am not disposed to tell you all that I foresee. It would be useless, it would frighten you..."

orientation. He says that "it is not that man happens to be disoriented, to be losing himself in life,
but that, insofar as one can see, man's situation,
his life, in itself *is* disorientation, is being lost."[5]
In the face of this, there is a deep need for human
beings to unify their experience into a narrative
that gives clarity to these experiences. This need
is so fundamental that Gasset says it exists
whether one wills to feel it or not. It is an "immediate necessity …[something] having its roots in
me, indigenous, autochthonous, authentic."[6] Not
every one of these narratives is authentic, though.
Gasset talks about "imposed" stories. These are
ideologies imposed on humans when they actually have no interest or need for such stories.[7] The

---

[5] Ortega y Gasset, *Some Lessons in Metaphysics*,
27.

[6] Ibid., 16.

[7] Ibid., 23. "… there is introduced into the human
mind a foreign body, a set of dead ideas that could not
be assimilated. This culture, which does not have any
root structure in man, a culture which does not spring
from him spontaneously, lacks any native and indigenous values; this is something imposed, extrinsic,
strange, foreign, and unintelligible; in short, it is un-
real. Underneath the culture - received but not truly

authentic narrative is one that deals with the most universal and inescapable questions, not some lesser set of ideas.[8] Philosophy, then, is born as an attempt by man to understand his situation in the midst of disparate complexity. Man pushes out into the dark and with each step casts the shadows of the unknown further and further away.

Creating a Philosophical Framework, the Sub-soil of Belief

This pushing out into the dark consists of confronting two fundamental questions. First, it is to ask the question *"What is it?"*[9] What is the

---

assimilated - man will remain intact as he was; that is to say, he will remain uncultured, a barbarian."

[8] Ibid.,16. "Well now, when man sees himself obliged to accept an external and mediate need, he finds himself in an equivocal, ambivalent situation, because this is the same as being invited to make his own (which means to accept) a necessity which is not his. Whether he likes it or not, he must behave as though it were his; he is thus invited to share in a fiction, a falsehood, a deception. And although this man may put forth all his good will in order to feel as if it were his, this does not mean that he achieves this, nor is it even probable that he can."

[9] Ibid., 29.

nature of being itself? Second, it is to ask what it means to even be a conscious knower of being. As confusing as the world outside man is, just as confusing is the inward turn attempting to understand himself. There, too, is chaos and disorientation regarding man's identity. He must find some orientation regarding his origin, identity, and purpose in life.[10]

> "To feel oneself lost! Did you ever consider what those words mean in themselves? Without going beyond them, to feel oneself lost implies first the sensation of feeling oneself-- that is, meeting oneself, finding oneself; but, by the same token, that self which man encounters on feeling himself consists precisely in a pure state of being lost."[11]

It is this identity which then colors everything else about the human search for truth. It is all part of one's life, what one does and what happens to someone. In this context, one begins to

---

[10] Ibid., 30-1.
[11] Ibid., 31.

form an orienting narrative for themselves.[12] This orienting narrative, or worldview, is that which gives a framework to all the actions that a person takes and strives for. It is the interpretative structure of the individual's life as a whole.[13] It is these most basic attitudes toward reality that make up the "sub-soil" on which one's beliefs rest.[14]

> "[T]his primary ignorance, this fundamental not knowing, is a not knowing what to do. This is what forces us to frame for ourselves an idea of things and of ourselves, to find out 'what there is' in reality, so that we may be able, in view of the image which the Universe presents to us as 'being what in truth it is,' to project our conduct with certainty, that is,

---

[12] Ibid., 36.

[13] Ortega y Gasset, *The Idea of Principle in Leibnitz and the Evolution of Deductive Theory,* 271. "Philosophy is a system of basic interpretive, and therefore intellectual, attitudes which man adopts in view of what is, for him, the tremendous event of finding himself alive. This life of his includes not only the event of his own existence but also a whole world of other events which are part of his life."

[14] Ibid., 271.

with sufficient meaning, and to emerge from
that primary ignorance.[15]

To tinker with the sub-soil of society's most
fundamental beliefs is to directly manipulate the
realm of human action. If one somehow destroys
the fundamental narrative, then the disorienting
complexity returns, and people are paralyzed
without any direction in which to act. One would
be able to manipulate people's actions by giving
them a new context in which to seek and strive.[16]
Thus, the Western philosophical journey was begun through the seeking of an orienting story.

The Philosophical Conversation of the West[17]

Now Gasset does mention that even before
philosophy took up this role to provide a world-

---

[15] Ibid., 272.

[16] Ibid.

[17] Ortega y Gasset, *The Origin of Philosophy*, "... all
philosophies have a very good mutual understanding
of one another: they constitute a conversation that has
lasted for nearly three millenniums, a perpetual dialogue and dispute held in a common tongue, namely
the philosophical viewpoint itself and the perennial
existence of the same difficult problems."

view in which man could function, religion played a similar role before it. For example, as religion began to wane in Ancient Greece, philosophy became a way forward that was clearer and clearer to people.[18] Since then, philosophy has been a continual conversation about the best story of reality. It is a conversation that has lasted for two and a half thousand years. This conversation between thinkers and among generations is a type of dialectic in which ideas are explored, reacted to, and synthesized.[19] Philosophy is a "perpetual dialogue" in which the search for truth goes through a continual dialectic of purification.[20] There are errors along the way, but the next generation can remove them and start with the rest as their new foundation.[21] These incomplete glimpses of truth Gasset calls "aspects" of philosophy. Being is so complex that even the simplest object will produce an almost endless supply of novel interactions and facets of itself.

---

[18] Ortega y Gasset, *The Idea of Principle in Leibnitz and the Evolution of Deductive Theory,* 273-74.

[19] Ortega y Gasset, *The Origin of Philosophy,* 14-9.

[20] Ibid., 47-8.

[21] Ibid., 25-31.

That is part of the reason that philosophy is a continual process. Man must often return to being,
interacting with it anew each time, learning each
time.[22]

The growing unity in the rational mind produced in one's knowledge of the identity of the
thing is a sign that there is likewise an identity of
being within the thing itself. This unity Gasset
calls a thing's "metaphysical entirety." He writes,

> "[M]etaphysical phenomen[a] . . . are not
> mysterious or supernatural, but of the sim-
> plest, most ordinary and everyday order - are
> the truest phenomena or 'facts' in existence,
> having precedence over all 'scientific facts,'
> which assume the existence of the former."[23]

---

[22] Ibid., 39. "This scene [looking at the wall] would
be reproduced indefinitely if he continued to gaze at
the wall indefinitely, the latter, like an inexhaustible
spring of reality, would keep issuing forth unsuspected
contents in a never-ending process of self-revelation."

[23] Ibid., 42-3.

This does not mean that one has the metaphysical entirety. One cannot, but one acquires aspects of it in the continual exploration of philosophy.[24]

Over time a common set of questions arises; one to which each age and each philosophical system returns. Though there may be different opinions in answering the questions, nevertheless, the questions manifest themselves as perennial.[25]

"[D]espite the existence of many divergent opinions, all are opinions on the same thing. This invites us to try to detect amid the multitude of philosophies some unity, and even a oneness in philosophy; to discover what the diverse doctrines have in common ... that all possess ultimately a unity."[26]

For those on the cutting edge of discovery, they uncover being in such a novel way that no language has yet been created to express it. It is found in its "ontological rawness."[27] Philosophy

---

[24] Ibid., 45-6.
[25] Ibid., 52-3.
[26] Ibid., 53.
[27] Ibid., 60.

is spurred along as it seeks to fashion linguistic tools through which to capture the essence of what has been experienced. It is first the poet who must bridge the gap between experience and language, but eventually words become concretized. This, too, can be perilous if it becomes so concrete that the original experience is lost. Philosophy must go back and revisit those original experiences and poetic expressions of being in its rawness. To philosophize is to pull back the veil of the obvious and peer into the depths of being. It is to undress reality and behold its nakedness. It is a living experience of reality, not a dead letter or concretized term.[28] In the continual pursuit of the deepest identity in things, the possibility of a formalized metaphysics is able to be born.

The Possibility of Metaphysics

From this background of how philosophy arises in human existence, it is now clear that philosophy is not reducible to the history of ideas. To philosophize is an activity that transcends specific times and places. It is an act with its own unique

---

[28] Ibid., 61-3.

essence, different from scientific investigation.
Now this does not mean that history or time does
not play a role in the act of philosophizing. There
is always a dual principle to the act in that, like
matter and form, eternal ideas are understood in
the historical situation in which they have pene-
trated man's consciousness, a particular time and
place. Philosophy is the conformity of man's
mind with eternal truths, allowing him to increase in his own being. Gasset coined the term
"perspectivism" to describe this reality. Perspectivism is to understand oneself as being in a historical situation yet encountering eternal truths.
With this awareness, man juxtaposes the existing
ideas of the time to those which were known in
the past.[29] It is a disposition of a particular age toward the unchanging and eternal, being more or
less open to it. In other words, it is something like
the worldview of the age.[30] Gasset recognizes the

---

[29] Ortega y Gasset, *What is Philosophy?*, 28.

[30] Ibid., 21. "This fragility gives truths a double
condition which is exceedingly curious. In themselves
they exist forever, without alteration or modification.
Yet their acquisition by a real person, subject to time,
gives them an aspect that is historical; they surge forth
on one date, and they may disappear on another.

shortcomings of worldviews in that the given ax-
ioms which form the mind of the age may be incomplete. Unlike Nietzsche, however, who took
this to mean that the idea of truth itself was subject to preferences of the age, Gasset claims that it
is a reality that transcends all historical worldviews. This is what philosophy seeks.[31]

> "[E]ach era, or more precisely each genera-
> tion, takes as its point of departure a set of as-
> sumptions which are more or less different
> from those that went before or will come af-
> ter, this means that the prevailing system of
> truths and values - esthetic, moral, political,
> or religious - has an inexorable dimension in

Clearly this temporal quality does not affect them, but
it does affect their presence in the human mind. What
really happens in time is the psychic act with which we
think about them; this is a real event, and effective
change in the flow of moments. It is the fact of our
knowing these truths, or being ignorant of them,
which has a history. And it is this which is mysterious
and disquieting, for it means that by virtue of one of
our thoughts, a transitory and fugitive reality in a most
fugitive world, we enter into possession of something
that is permanent and super-temporal."

[31] Ibid., 49-50.

terms of history; these are related to a certain vital human chronology, they have value for certain men, and nothing more. Truth is historical. How truth can, and indeed must, claim nevertheless to be super-historical- not relative but absolute - is the great question.[32]

In this regard, Gasset critiques the worldview of Materialism as incomplete. Each of the physical sciences only observe reality under given conditions, within the parameters of experiments and the limitations of its own discipline. Gasset claims that each expert ends up creating a metaphysics of their own discipline to fill in the absent data upon which their work rests. This is precisely why one must not pursue being within some particular aspect, but philosophy must pursue being *as such*. It must avoid the "idolatrous worship of the experiment" and seek the deeper principle of unity. In other words, it must answer the question, *"What is it?"* Philosophy is, properly speaking, metaphysics. It is to attempt to consider the universe a whole, as a unified reality, one which man is naturally drawn towards. It is an attempt

---

[32] Ibid.

to get at the ultimate principle of identity and unity in things.[33] This desire of unification is not something optional. Every person, conscious of it or not, will fill in the missing pieces in their understanding of the universe in order that they may have a framework of action.[34] This also includes a stance on the universe's first cause. In other words, every person has a worldview.[35]

---

[33] Ibid., 61-2. "[W]e do not know what that 'everything there is' may be; the only thing we think is a negative concept, namely the negation of that which would only be a part, a piece, a fragment. So the philosopher, in contradistinction to every other scientist, sets sail for the unknown as such. The more or less known is a part, a portion, a splinter of the Universe. The philosopher sets himself in front of his object in an attitude which is different from that of any other expert."

[34] Ortega y Gasset, *The Origin of Philosophy*, 75. "Religion, philosophy, and literature, vital functions of the human mind, appear as permanent possibilities in man. ... Otherwise we could not talk about mankind, human life, the human being. In other words, man has an invariable structure which traverses all of his changes."

[35] Ortega y Gasset, *What is Philosophy?*, 66. "The past century tried very hard to rein in the human mind and hold it in check within the limits set by exactness.

Gasset also makes the point, devastating to the materialist, that science itself was born from the Christian worldview. In fact, behind the scientist stands a person with his or her own worldview, often taking as self-evident the assumptions that science will be used for "the good" and that physical exactitude is equivalent with truth.[36] In Gasset's words, "The popular tendency to consider exactitude as an attribute which affects the value of truth lacks both justification and meaning."[37] Science does not come with an intrinsic value system.[38]

This violence, this turning the back on ultimate problems was called 'agnosticism.' Such an effort is neither justified nor plausible. That experimental science may be incapable of resolving those fundamental questions in its own way is no reason why it should behave like the fox with the high-hung grapes, should call them 'myths' and invite us to abandon them. How can we live deaf to the last, dramatic questions? Where does the world come from, wither is it going? What is the definitive power in the cosmos? What is the essential meaning of life? Confined to a zone of intermediate and secondary themes, we cannot breathe."

[36] Ibid., 72-4.

[37] Ibid., 72.

[38] Ibid., 67. "It is not escapable. One cannot simply abandon the perennial questions of existence. What I

This is also where Gasset's defense of metaphysics comes in from his unique existentialist
perspective. He poses the question of why humans have a desire to move beyond physical appearance in the search for the metaphysical identity in things if there were no corresponding reality within humans which was akin to it? It is a
deeply ingrained existential longing which tor-
tures him, in a sense as though it were a phantom
limb.[39] Another way to express it would be as a
stomach longs for food yet is told that food does
not exist. It would never arise as a genuine problem if it did not actually exist.[40] [41]

---

mean by this is that we are given no escape from the
ultimate questions. Whether we like it nor not, they
live, in one fashion or another, within us. 'Scientific
truth' is exact, but it is incomplete and penultimate; it
is of necessity, embedded in another kind of truth,
complete and ultimate, although inexact, which could
be called 'myth.' Scientific truth floats, then, in mythology, and science itself, as a whole, is a myth, the admi-
rable European myth."

[39] Ibid., 70.

[40] Ibid., 82.

[41] Ibid., 70. "Only Plato glimpsed the fact that the
root knowing, its very substance we might say, lies in
the insufficiency of human powers, in the terrible fact
that man 'does not know.' Neither God nor animal is

Here Gasset introduces a novel look at traditional metaphysics. He argues that a new way of
looking at the problem is not to continue to look
deeper into the nature of *things*, but *people*. This
is what he terms the "ante-physical." The ante-
physical is the worldview that every person has,
whether they are conscious of it or not, in order
to create a complete picture of reality.[42] Now this
does not take away the mysterious nature of the
metaphysical. Gasset says that at the same time
the philosopher sets out for a unified understanding of all that is, he is aware he may never penetrate that mystery to his satisfaction. Scientific
utilitarianism may numb people to the pursuit,
may provide human beings with practicalities
clearer to them, but it will never satisfy the desire
to know what is most real, what is farthest from
the human mind. This is clearly where humans

---

in this condition. God knows everything, and therefore feels no need to know. The animals know nothing.
But man is the living insufficient one. Man needs to
know, he is desperately aware that he is ignorant. This
is what it is useful to analyze. Why does man's ignorance hurt him, how can he feel the ache in a member
he never had?"

[42] Ibid., 74.

are not equivalent to animals. Animals have practical problems that they are aware of yet never
seek to transcend them. Animals have no existential crises. The human has no such bliss of ignorance but must set out into the unknown on the
philosopher's quest for that which is ultimate.[43]

"It is knowledge carried to its maximum effort; it is intellectual heroism. The philosopher leaves nothing beneath his feet to serve
as a comfortable support, as unshakable terra
firma. He renounces all previous security,
puts himself into absolute peril, practices the
sacrifice of all his ingenious beliefs, commits
suicide as a live man [to] be reborn as if trans-
figured into pure exercise of the intellect."[44]

Gasset views the Scholastic formulation of
truth, as the conformity between the mind and reality, as a sign of hope in this philosophical journey. This is because if there were no qualitative
similarity between the structure of the mind and

---

[43] Ibid., 76-83.
[44] Ibid., 84.

the nature of things, then there would exist no intelligibility. That is, nothing could be known rationally at all. The reality of intelligibility reflects
a deeper nature to things and gives an indication
that all of reality must be likewise intelligible,
even if it is difficult to pursue. It is, likewise, difficult to obtain the intelligibility of pure reason in
things which are more deeply embedded in material parts.[45] Gasset proposes a middle way of intelligibility to the philosophical pursuit of *"What
is it?"* with the term "vital-reason." Vital reason is
a search for the metaphysical, but a search that
recognizes the mysterious nature of being, not
seeking to tame it improperly. Gasset is not eager
to return to an overtly stated or dogmatic version
of metaphysics which ends up reducing the mystery of being in its attempt to understand it.[46] He

---

[45] Ibid., 85-7. "For me, this is a classic example of
what I call intellectual utopism, that is to say, the made
faith that thought, when it wishes to penetrate the real
at almost any spot -u-topos- on its infinite body will
find that body transparent and coinciding with
thought itself. If this is so, I need not wait to find the
unknown real; having anticipated it, I know how it will
behave."

[46] Ortega y Gasset, *The Origin of Philosophy*, 67-8.
"...behind the strange divergent landscapes and fauna

explains, "it would hardly be intelligent to interpret the definition of philosophy as a doctrine of the Universe, and the tendency to construct a maximum of philosophic corpus as an ingenuous lapse into the old metaphysics."[47]

In conclusion, it is clear that despite the attempt of new materialist worldviews to supplant Metaphysical Theism, it is ultimately impossible. There is an aspect of reality which, though mysterious, will always haunt man. He can try to ignore it. He can try to explain it away. He can try to remove it by force of will or manipulation, but it is the most real aspect of reality there is, and it will perennially return to his consciousness.

---

just presented by the mass of philosophies, we are now able to discern the persistent existence of two worlds, the manifest world and the latent or supra-world. The latent world pulsates beneath the manifest world and its revelation constitutes the supreme philosophical task. ...philosophy is not content with one world, the habitual one, but divides or superimpregnates it, compels us to shuttle across the dividing line which, like a frontier, separates philosophy's 'outside' from its 'inside,' its outer image from its innermost essential condition, its interiority."

[47] Ortega y Gasset, *What is Philosophy?*, 89-90.

Chapter IV

Transhumanism:
The Worldview of the Future

This study concludes with a final chapter that offers some heuristic value and insight into the future. As time progresses, and Materialism becomes more powerful through its development of technology and aid to man's bodily existence, it seems inevitable that the irreconcilable abyss between Materialism and Metaphysical Theism will become more and more pronounced. How will people of these worldviews coexist within a shared society when the fundamental premises of both are diametrically opposed?[1] This is a serious question which needs to be answered soon.

---

[1] Second Vatican Council, On The Apostolate of the Laity in Environments Imbued with Materialism, Particularly Marxism *De Apostolatu Laicorum* (April 1962). in Acta et Documenta Concilio Oecumenico Vaticano II Apparando, Series II (Praeparatoria),

As Dostoyevsky argued in *The Possessed*, it only takes three generations for society to be radically changed.[2] How fierce will the conflicts of the future be if just the first round of conflict between these worldviews brought destruction on a mass scale? In the words of the Catholic Cardinal Francis George from 2010, "I expect to die in bed,

---

trans. Matthew Hoffman (*Lifesite News*, 2017). 345 - 348. "Among those nations that are principally Christian, practical materialism is growing ever more extensive, is strengthening, and is making a covert entrance into people's consciences. So-called "Marxism," which professes an open and militant atheism, must be regarded as the preeminent form of this materialism, which engages in a systematic effort to advance its doctrines principally – although not exclusively – among the workers, but also among the elites. … While Marxism, which Pope Pius XII personally reprobates and condemns, is the most grave form of materialism and the one most hostile towards the Christian faith, it is yet not the only form of modern materialism. In this day, there are many men who, although they openly profess themselves to be Christians, passively consent to the daily course of events, identify human happiness with technological and economic progress, covet riches, strive to construct a world based on them, and gradually withdraw themselves from God, whom they remove little by little from their own lives."

[2] Dostoyevsky, *The Possessed*, 450.

my successor will die in prison and his successor will die a martyr in the public square."[3] If we end his thought right there, we find it resembles Dostoyevsky's three generations of social degradation, but three bishops can change in a single generation. While man is currently tamed by the biological barriers of reality which limit his desires, as technology continues to rapidly develop, it will soon provide us with the power, for a time, at least, to fundamentally change the identity of Western society in almost every respect. Consider the following examples below.

The Promethean Temptation of Technology

In the 1990's, Pope John Paul II gave a warning to the modern world in his encyclical *Evangelium Vitae.* He warned about the growing temptation for man to usurp the place of God through the power of technology. Just as Prometheus stole fire from the gods in Ancient Greek mythology, John Paul II identified the desire to have control

---

[3] Tim Drake, "Cardinal George: The Myth and Reality of 'I'll Die in My Bed'." *The National Catholic Register*, April 17, 2015, at www.ncregister.com.

of life and death as man's conscious, or even unconscious, striving in the modern world.[4] For all
human history, man's desires were relatively
bounded by the barriers of biology. Life, death,
marriage, reproduction, family, medicine, and
the like were all realities that were subject to the
natural order of things. Currently, and certainly
into the future, technology is attempting to transcend every biological barrier that once limited
man in these domains. In-Vitro Fertilization
technology, combined with surrogacy, has redefined the meaning of family. Contraceptives have
redefined the meaning of sex from something tied
to procreation into its own separate activity of
pleasure. Growing experimental surgeries, and
fields of psychology, are trying to redefine the traditional binary male-female notion of gender. Experiments with combining human and animal
DNA,[5] creating types of human animal hybrids,

---

[4] Pope John Paul II, Encyclical on the Value and
Inviolability of Human Life *Evangelium Vitae* (25
March 1995), §16.

[5] Rob Stein, "Scientists Create Early Embryos That
Are Part Human, Part Monkey." National Public Radio, 2021. At https://www.npr.org/sections/health-

are redefining the meaning of human.[6] Artificial wombs, or "bio-bags," may redefine what birth looks like, as someone could be conceived and gestated to birth in a laboratory.[7] There may come a point where a man could produce his own child by repurposing a cell from his own body into an embryo ready to receive his own sperm.[8] Experiments with gene manipulation and augmentation may create an inseparable barrier be-

---

shots/2021/04/15/987164563/scientists-create-early-embryos-that-are-part-human-part-monkey.

[6] Michelle Roberts, "Man Gets Genetically-Modified Pig Heart in World-First Transplant." BBC News, January 11, 2022, at www.BBC.com.

[7] Jenny Kleeman, "'Parents Can Look at Their Foetus in Real Time': Are Artificial Wombs the Future?" *The Guardian*, 2020. Online at https://www.theguardian.com/lifeandstyle/2020/jun/27/parents-can-look-foetus-real-time-artificial-wombs-future.

[8] The Telegraph, "All Sperm, No Eggs: Motherless Babies on the Way, Say Scientists." *National Post*, 2016. At https://nationalpost.com/ news/world/all-sperm-no-eggs-motherless-babies-on-the-way-say-scientists

tween those who have the money for their children and those who do not.[9] These developments are all part of a larger movement known as "Transhumanism." Transhumanism is the in-between stage of humanity between current humanity, frustrated by so many aspects of reality, and "Posthumanity," a humanity totally freed from suffering and death and able to enjoy the ceaseless pleasures of life through the power of technology, in order

> "to be resistant to disease and impervious to aging; to have unlimited youth and vigor; to exercise control over their own desires, moods, and mental states; to be able to avoid feeling tired, hateful, or irritated about petty things; to have an increased capacity for pleasure, love, artistic appreciation, and serenity; to experience novel states of consciousness that current human brains cannot access. It seems likely that the simple fact of

---

[9] Kashyap Vyas, "Designer Babies: Gene-Editing and the Controversial Use of CRISPR." *Interesting Engineering Magazine,* 2019. Online at https://interestingengineering.com/designer-babies-gene-editing-and-the-controversial-use-of-crispr

living an indefinitely long, healthy, active life would take anyone to posthumanity if they went on accumulating memories, skills, and intelligence. [10]

By merging humans with machines in various ways, the human person would become something quite distinct from the previous age of humans.[11] If this was not disconcerting enough, some claim that many will remove themselves from a physical body altogether and reside solely

---

[10] "What is Transhumanism?" At Transhumanism FAQ Version 3.0, at www.whatistranshumanism.org.

[11] "What is Transhumanism?" "Posthumans could be completely synthetic artificial intelligences, or they could be enhanced uploads ... or they could be the result of making many smaller but cumulatively profound augmentations to a biological human. The latter alternative would probably require either the redesign of the human organism using advanced nanotechnology or its radical enhancement using some combination of technologies such as genetic engineering, psycho-pharmacology, anti-aging therapies, neural interfaces, advanced information management tools, memory enhancing drugs, wearable computers, and cognitive techniques."

within the virtual world as an artificial consciousness. Whether this is ever possible, or not, can be
debated, but it is a reflection of the ultimate aspi-
rations of the materialist worldview. Kirilov was
right; it is to create heaven on earth. [12]

The Black Mirror of the Virtual World

While it may seem far-fetched to speak of an
artificial consciousness, there is certainly a growing trend for humanity to live more of their lives
within the virtual reality sphere than actual reality. In doing this, man may obscure, yet again, his

---

[12] "What is Transhumanism?" "Some posthumans
may find it advantageous to jettison their bodies altogether and live as information patterns on vast super-
fast computer networks. Their minds may be not only
more powerful than ours but may also employ different cognitive architectures or include new sensory mo-
dalities that enable greater participation in their virtual
reality settings. Posthuman minds might be able to
share memories and experiences directly, greatly in-
creasing the efficiency, quality, and modes in which
posthumans could communicate with each other. The
boundaries between posthuman minds may not be as
sharply defined as those between humans."

desire for the metaphysical. A regular mirror reflects one's image back to them as it is in reality. To see oneself in the mirror can often be a sign of introspection and self-searching, a journey to one's deepest identity. Technology, though, is the black mirror of an artificial screen. It does not reflect the deep reality of oneself back to them, but a distorted virtual image.[13] As every moment and event is recorded by technology, as people's lives are spent in the virtual world, they may feel as though they are experiencing reality. It is a simulation, though, a perverted copy. Living life through virtual technology is a distortion of the true human experience. To ask the first philosophical question, *"What is it?"*, reveals that it is almost nothing at all. It is a pseudo experience. In the virtual world, man is already fully God. It is the worldview of the future because, to those who

---

[13] Arcade Fire, "Black Mirror," from *Neon Bible*. Merge Records, 2007, MP4 audio file, iTunes. "I walked down to the ocean after waking from a nightmare. No moon, no pale reflection. Black mirror, black mirror. Shot by a security camera, you cannot watch your own image and also look yourself in the eye. Black mirror, black mirror, black mirror. I know a time is coming, all words will lose their meaning."

submit themselves to its realm, there is no belief or truth outside of what those who control the technology dictate. [14]

---

[14] Nietzsche, *Beyond Good and Evil,* 85. "Whoever battles with monsters had better see that it does not turn him into a monster. And if you gaze long into an abyss, the abyss will gaze back at you."

Conclusion

This study has been an exploration into the power that worldviews wield over human societies. Worldviews are the stories within which individual humans operate and live their lives in order to shelter themselves from paralyzing complexity. Only by having a narrative which provides a clear origin, identity, and purpose can man act and live together with others. Otherwise, there will inevitably be conflict. It has also been argued in this thesis that worldviews are the result of how a society answers the fundamental philosophical question, *"What is it?"* This question represents the most basic choice in the way one views reality, either for or against the existence of the metaphysical. The drama of the history of philosophy directly reflects the answer given by each generation. This drama was certainly seen in the 19th and 20th centuries with the birth of materialist worldviews that rejected the metaphysical and sought to create a whole new world order in which humanity would take up its future.

Through the work of Jose Ortega y Gasset, it has been argued that the metaphysical identity in being can never be stamped out, only suppressed for a time before it perennially returns to human consciousness. If the metaphysical is real, then materialist worldviews will only succeed in implementing themselves through force, using the tactics of physical terror and ideological manipulation. The destructive events of the 20th century have been given at least a partial explanation, then, in that such devastating coercion was exactly what took place.

Finally, this book concluded with a look at Transhumanism as the logical conclusion of the worldview of Materialism. The denial of metaphysical reality only transfers man's desires for ultimate fulfillment here to this earth, to be fulfilled with the power of technology by breaking down every biological barrier that hinders man's desires. This represents a serious warning to Theists. It will only become harder and harder for Theists and materialists to exist together as there are fewer and fewer shared beliefs. Alienation and conflict may be imminent. Yet, because of the ultimate indestructibility of metaphysical reality, humanity is not without hope. It is necessary to conclude this thesis with the full version of Cardinal George's quote. "I expect to die in bed, my successor will die in prison and his successor will die a martyr in the public square. *His successor will pick up the shards of a ruined society and slowly help rebuild civilization, as the church has done so often in human history.*"[1]

---

[1] Tim Drake, "Cardinal George: The Myth and Reality of 'I'll Die in My Bed'." *The National Catholic Register*, April 17, 2015, at www.ncregister.com.

Bibliography

Arcade Fire. "Black Mirror," from *Neon Bible*. Merge Records, 2007, MP4 audio file, iTunes.

Arendt, Hannah. *The Origins of Totalitarianism*. New York: Harcourt, 1970.

Arendt, Hannah. "The Great Tradition and the Nature of Totalitarianism." Lecture at New School for Social Research, 1953. At Https://Memory.loc.gov/Ammem/Arendthtml/mharendtFolderP05.Html

Arendt, Hannah. "Totalitarianism." Lecture at Oberlin College, Oberlin, Ohio, 28 October 1954. At www.memory.loc.gov/ammem/arendthtml/arendthome.html

Yuri Bezmenov, interview by G. Edward Griffin, "Soviet Subversion of the Free World Press," 1984, At American Media, https://youtu.be/jMnhSBySKto

Campbell, Joseph. *Thou Art That, Transforming Religious Metaphor*. Novato, California: New World Library, 2001.

Copleston, Frederick. *A History of Philosophy Volume VIII: Modern Philosophy Empiricism, Idealism, and Pragmatism in Britain and America*. New York: Doubleday, 1994.

Darwin, Charles. *The Descent of Man*. London: Penguin Books, 2004.

De Lubac, Henri. *The Drama of Atheist Humanism*. San Francisco: Ignatius, 1998.

Dewey, John. *Experience and Nature*. Mccutchen Press, 2011. Kindle.

Dewey, John. *Quest For Certainty*. of *Twentieth-Century Philosophy*. Upper Saddle River, NJ: Prentice Hall, 2003.

Dewey, John. *The Influence of Darwin on Philosophy and Other Essays*. New York: Henry Holt and Company, 1910. Online at http://www.brocku.ca/MeadProject/Dewey/Dewey_1910b/Dewey_1910)01.html.

Discovery Science. "Darwin, Africa, and Genocide: The Horror of Scientific Racism." YouTube video, from Discovery Institute. Posted by Discovery Science on 7 July 2020, at https://youtu.be/ lQPrvPM38Ws

Dostoyevsky, Fyodor. *Crime and Punishment*. New York: Vintage Books, 1950.

Dostoyevsky, Fyodor. *The Possessed.* A Public Domain Book. Kindle.

Drake, Tim. "Cardinal George: The Myth and Reality of 'I'll Die in My Bed'." *The National Catholic Register*, April 17, 2015, at www.ncregister.com.

Fieser, James and Samuel Stumpf. *Philosophy: A Historical Survey with Essential Readings 10th Edition.* New York: McGraw Hill Education, 2020.

Hedges, Chris. "What Every Person Should Know About War." *The New York Times* (NY), July 6, 2003, 11:00 p.m. EST, What to Read. at www.nytimes.com.

Human Zoos, America's Forgotten History of Scientific Racism. Directed by John G. West. Seattle, WA: Discovery Institute, 2018.

Huxley, Thomas. *Evolution and Ethics.* Fairfield, IA: 1st World Library, 2003.

Kleeman, Jenny. "'Parents Can Look at Their Foetus in Real Time': Are Artificial Wombs the Future?". The Guardian, 2020. At https://www.theguardian.com/life-andstyle/2020/jun/27/parents-can-look-foetus-real-time-artificial-wombs-future.

Kung, Hans. *Does God Exist? An Answer For To-day*. New York: Doubleday & Company, 1980.

Marx, Karl. "Theses on Feuerbach." *In Economic and Philosophic Manuscripts of 1844*. Prep. Institute of Marxism-Leninism. Moscow: Foreign Languages Publishing House, 1956.

Marx, Karl. "Critique of Hegel's Philosophy of Right." In *Karl Marx: Early Writings*. Trans. and Ed. by T.B. Bottomore. McGraw Hill. NY, 1963.

Marx, Karl. "Critique of the Hegelian Dialectic and Philosophy as a Whole." In *Economic and Philosophic Manuscripts of* 1844: Prep. Institute of Marxism-Leninism, 142-171. Moscow: Foreign Languages Publishing House, 1956.

Meyer, Stephen. "The Return of the God Hypothesis." *Journal of Interdisciplinary Studies*, no. 11 (1999): 1-38.

Miller, James. *Examined Lives: From Socrates to Nietzsche*. New York: Picador, 2012.

Moreno, Antonio. *Jung, Gods, and Modern Man*. Notre Dame, Indiana: University of Notre Dame Press, 1970.

Nietzsche, Friedrich. *Beyond Good and Evil*. Chicago: Henry Regnery Company, 1955.

Nietzsche, Friedrich. *Beyond Good and Evil*. of *Philosophy: A Historical Survey With Essential Readings 10th Edition*. New York: McGraw Hill Education, 2020.

Nietzsche, Friedrich. *Genealogy of Morals*. Series Five Book 24 of *Delphi Complete Works of Friedrich Nietzsche*. United Kingdom: Delphi Classics, 2015. Kindle.

Nietzsche, Friedrich. *Twilight of the Idols*. Series Five Book 24 of *Delphi Complete Works of Friedrich Nietzsche*. United Kingdom: Delphi Classics, 2015. Kindle.

Ortega y Gasset, Jose. *Some Lessons in Metaphysics*. New York: W.W. Norton Company, 1969.

Ortega y Gasset, Jose. *The Idea of Principle in Leibnitz and the Evolution of Deductive Theory*. New York: W.W. Norton Company, 1971.

Ortega y Gasset, Jose. *The Origin of Philosophy*. New York: W.W. Norton Company, 1967.

Ortega y Gasset, Jose. *What is Philosophy?* New York: W.W. Norton Company, 1960.

Peterson, Jordan. *Maps of Meaning: The Architecture of Belief.* New York: Routledge, 1998.

Pope John Paul II. Encyclical on The Relationship Between Faith and Reason *Fides et Ratio* (14 September 1998).

Pope John Paul II. Encyclical on the Value and Inviolability of Human Life *Evangelium Vitae* (25 March 1995).

Ratzinger, Joseph Cardinal. *Introduction to Christianity.* San Francisco: Ignatius Press, 2004.

Roberts, Michelle. "Man Gets Genetically-Modified Pig Heart in World-First Transplant." BBC News, January 11, 2022, at www.BBC.com.

Sarah, Cardinal Robert and Nicholas Diat. *The Day is Now Far Spent.* Ignatius Press. San Francisco, 2019.

Second Vatican Council, On the Apostolate of the Laity in Environments Imbued with Materialism, Particularly Marxism *De Apostolatu Laicorum* (April 1962). in *Acta et Documenta Concilio Oecumenico Vaticano II Apparando*, Series II (Praeparatoria), trans. Matthew Hoffman, Lifesite News, 2017.

Solzhenitsyn, Aleksandr. *One Day in the Life of Ivan Denisovich.* New York: Frederick A. Praeger, 1963.

Solzhenitsyn, Aleksandr. *The Gulag Archipelago, 1918-1956 An Experiment in Literary Investigation I-II.* New York: Harper and Row Publishers, 1974.

Rob Stein. "Scientists Create Early Embryos That Are Part Human, Part Monkey." National Public Radio, 2021. At https://www.npr.org/sections/health-shots/2021/04/15/987164563/scientists-create-early-embryos-that-are-part-human-part-monkey.

The Telegraph. "All Sperm, No Eggs: Motherless Babies on the Way, Say Scientists." National Post, 2016. At https://nationalpost.com/news/world/all-sperm-no-eggs-motherless-babies-on-the-way-say-scientists

Timeline - World History Documentaries. "How An American TV Crew Tracked Down a Nazi. Nazi Hunters." YouTube video, from Timeline - World History Documentaries. Posted by Timeline - World History Documentaries on 3 October 2021. Online at https://youtu.be/ hu42C7rinEU

Vyas, Kashyap. "Designer Babies: Gene-Editing and the Controversial Use of CRISPR." Interesting Engineering Magazine, 2019. At https://interestingengineering.com/designer-babies-gene-editing-and-the-controversial-use-of-crispr.

"What is Transhumanism?" At Transhumanism FAQ Version 3.0, at www.whatistranshumanism.org.

Wojtyla, Karol. *Love and Responsibility.* New York: Farrar-Straus-Giroux, 1981.

Made in the USA
Monee, IL
18 June 2024

59671329R00075